WHY ARE YOU HERE?

WHY ARE YOU HERE?

*Inspiration for living
the purpose-driven life*

DR. CLINTON A. VALLEY

Xulon Press
555 Winderley Pl, Suite 225
Maitland, FL 32751
407.339.4217
www.xulonpress.com

© 2023 by Dr. Clinton A. Valley

All rights reserved solely by the author. The author guarantees all contents are original and do not infringe upon the legal rights of any other person or work. No part of this book may be reproduced in any form without the permission of the author.

Due to the changing nature of the Internet, if there are any web addresses, links, or URLs included in this manuscript, these may have been altered and may no longer be accessible. The views and opinions shared in this book belong solely to the author and do not necessarily reflect those of the publisher. The publisher therefore disclaims responsibility for the views or opinions expressed within the work.

Unless otherwise indicated, Scripture quotations taken from the Contemporary English Version (CEV). Copyright © 1995 American Bible Society. Used by permission. All rights reserved.

Paperback ISBN-13: 978-1-66288-934-9
Ebook ISBN-13: 978-1-66288-935-6

Acknowledgments

This book is the fruition of my walk and talk with the Lord and His people over the past 50-plus years. It has been a joy to walk the Christian path and I have learnt so much, even more from the trials and challenges than from the outright successes and triumphs. I am deeply indebted to so many people who have contributed to the shaping of my Christian worldview as presented in this work.

First, I give thanks to God for calling me into His fellowship, into the ministry of the Seventh-day Adventist Church, and to be a lifelong Christian educator, now working in the public space. I also thank him for a wonderful Christian wife and the mother of our two lovely children, Clintelle and Clinson. We are also proud of the spouses our children have chosen, Timothy and Janet respectively, and our amazing grandsons, Caleb and Ethan. Martha has been a tower of emotional and spiritual strength to me over the years and has helped me to better understand what God is like. I can also think of so many who touched and blessed my life in special ways over the years and have provided further leaps in my understanding of the Christian experience, people like church leader Astor Dennis; sisters Agatha Williams and Daphne Garvin from Couva, Trinidad; and pastors Peter Prime, Stephen Purcell and K. S. Wiggins, based in Trinidad at the time. Some of these godly folks have passed to their rest, but their legacy lives on. These mentors nurtured my early faith and entry into the pastoral ministry. Dr. Walter Douglas at Andrews University and Pastors Cecil Perry, Don McFarlane and Orville Woolford were key luminaries in my British experience. Hamilton Williams, Theo Sargeant, and James Phillip were my early ministerial soulmates.

I also had the opportunity to minister and to interact with fellow Christians on the African continent. My good friend and ministerial colleague Pastor Nckeu Moses Msimanga from the Eastern Africa Division Headquarters in Harare, Zimbabwe has demonstrated to me the power of the transformed life in Christ. I have also been blessed to fellowship with the Mwinga family in Lusaka, Zambia, the young people from the Southern Africa Seventh-day Adventist Student Association, and the caring faculty and staff of the University of Eastern Africa in Eldoret, Kenya. I have treasured my experiences and associations from Africa. I continue to be associated with and blessed by our African brothers and sisters as I lead out at the Atlanta Abahiriwe Church in Clarkston, Georgia.

Also, I valued and appreciated the deep compassion and Spirit-filled Christian leadership of Pastor V. Mendinghall, former President of the South Atlantic Conference of Seventh-day Adventists in Atlanta, Georgia; current president, Pastor Calvin Preston; and our esteemed pastoral family friends, Lawrence and Brenda Hamilton, whom I have known for almost 30 years. More recently, I have been blessed to fellowship with ministerial colleagues in the Georgia Cumberland Conference. Thanks to Regional Director, Dr. Neil Reid, for opening this opportunity. Further, I have been enjoying my journey as a professor of educational leadership at the University of the Virgin Islands, and I am so appreciative of the support of the administration and faculty colleagues. In all the varied chapters of my life, I have seen the guiding hand of God – a God who loves, cares and protects. He is the One who provides meaning and purpose as to why I am here.

More directly in connection with the production of this work, I am truly grateful to Dr. Calvin Rock for taking the time to read the manuscript and for kindly consenting to write the foreword. Thanks also to the other colleagues and friends who read the manuscript and submitted their worthwhile comments. I believe that the Lord sent two dear ladies of great expertise into my path when this work was first published in 2000. Ms. Judy Willis provided an insightful critique of the manuscript and worked hard to transform me from the preacher to the writer. Ms. Akosua Betty Reedy of Dez-Tech Information Services worked relentlessly to ensure a quality product for the earlier publication, and I remain very grateful to her.

How do you acknowledge all the contributors in your life's drama? I have learnt so much from so many in so many ways that it is impossible to have an accurate roll call. This book is the product of all these learning adventures. Therefore, I just say thanks to all and to the God of us all who makes all things possible. Let us all look forward to the time when we would have an eternity to say, "Thank you."

Table of Contents

Acknowledgments vii
Foreword xiii
Introduction xv

Section One–To Live

Chapter 1. Why Are You Here? 3
Chapter 2. Living by Faith. 17
Chapter 3. Religion in Working Clothes. 29
Chapter 4. Partnership with God. 37

Section Two -To Love

Chapter 5. Love Must Be Tough. 47
Chapter 6. For Adults Only. 57
Chapter 7. Thank You 73
Chapter 8. The Returning Rebel. 79

Section Three–To Learn

Chapter 9. The Spirit of Overcomers. 95
Chapter 10. A Call to Excellence 105
Chapter 11. Your Winning Combination 113
Chapter 12. The Lost Treasure 125

Section Four -To Look

Chapter 13. The Modern Laodicean Church 137
Chapter 14. Fill me, Holy Spirit!. 147
Chapter 15. Trouble Won't Last 159
Chapter 16. From Vision to Victory 165

Table of Contents

Foreword

There is a plethora of devotional writings available on the shelves of bookstores at airports and Bible houses throughout the land. Not often, however, is life in the trenches of daily experience examined with such clear spiritual focus as is done on the pages that follow. Dr. Valley's broad experience as scholar, teacher, pastor/evangelist, administrator, writer and parent gives him special leverage for the counsel that these pages contain.

Why Are You Here? presents Bible-based guidance for young and old, marrieds and singles, clergy and lay persons, teachers and students, parents and children, believers and nonbelievers and Christians, new and experienced, in plain, practical terminology generously punctuated with memorable (often personal) case histories.

Because our stewardship requires us to make the most of our time and talents; because life is too short for any of it to be wasted following false trails or even wandering aimlessly on the right one; because so many false voices are today raised in constant competition for our attention, the focus upon worthy goals and right principles in these pages serves as welcome guideposts for every struggling, striving seeker of truth and success.

As you will discover, this book is from the heart of one whose journey with pain and sorrow, as well as victory and triumph, is shared with candor often spiced with humor that makes for good reading. By exposing to us his lifetime of living and learning, Dr. Valley gives us spiritual impetus for survival and growth well worth our noting and emulation.

No matter what one's stage or situation in life, the counsel, if heeded, will produce new energies, better priorities, keener focus, broader perceptions, higher principles, deeper understandings and, most importantly, an ever-enhanced, ever-improving walk with God.

Calvin B. Rock, Ph.D.
Former Vice President, General Conference of Seventh-day Adventists, Maryland, USA

Introduction

Let's call her Tessa. She was a happy-go-lucky, 18-year-old teenager in my congregation, Tessa attended church regularly but was on the fringes spiritually. At times she led in youth services and was absolutely brilliant, for she was a young lady with good organizational skills and great talent for speaking, singing, poetry and overall leadership. On the other hand, from time to time, she would attend parties and events where she would smoke cigarettes, consume alcohol, carouse with characters of questionable moral worth and generally disavow her Christian commitment and lifestyle.

In talking with Tessa, I began to learn of her escapades and sought to encourage her spiritually. Her father had left home, and she took that blow quite seriously. It was clear that she was in rebellion. Nevertheless, despite her sorry circumstances, I felt it was a tragedy for her to waste her amazing potential and so I took a personal interest in her. She became a friend of our family and would stay over at our home on occasions.

I challenged Tessa to think positively about her future. Life was more than transient fun, alcohol and drugs. "Why are you here, Tessa?" was an expression I would use frequently to help her focus on her reason for being and the need to fulfill some worthwhile purpose in her life. One day, I brought college admission applications to her and Angelica, her partner in frivolity. I encouraged both of them to think about starting college the following fall. Although they would have to start by obtaining their GEDs, I pointed out that with time and determination, they both had the potential to achieve Ph.Ds. Angelica's vision could not stretch that far, but interestingly, over time, Tessa began to believe that she could achieve success if she put her mind to it.

That fall, Tessa headed off to a Seventh-day Adventist college having just barely passed the GED entry requirements for that school. Angelica stayed at home. Tessa had her financial, emotional and spiritual struggles along the way, but she stayed in school and did well academically. After four years, she graduated with her BS degree and entered graduate school. Eventually, Tessa completed her Ph.D. in molecular biology and worked as a research scientist at an internationally renowned university. Thankfully, she also remained within the church fellowship. Angelica never took the GED and remained at home.

Tessa and Angelica have been the inspiration for this book. Why are you here? What on earth are you doing? I believe this is both a philosophical and practical question that every person must keep answering. I have had to deal with this question several times in my own life. When I sat in theology classes at Caribbean Union College, when I pursued a doctorate in education, when I looked through the window of my home on those cold, dark and wet wintry days in London, when I sat in the principal's chair at John Loughborough School dealing with some of the thorny issues in high school administration. Again, this was the question I asked myself several times during those challenging years as President of the University of the Southern Caribbean. At all these times I had to stop, take stock and prayerfully reassure myself that I was where God wanted me to be. For me, this question is a self-test for relevance and purpose. It is a call for a reflective pause along life's journey to take stock of where you are and why you are where you are. To fail to do this may make your life a chance, purposeless existence.

We are not mere, worthless pieces of protoplasm washed up on the shores of time, here today and gone tomorrow. Our life is not to be a discordant symphony without rhyme or reason. Too many people live their lives from day to day, functioning merely as a door on a hinge, going in and coming out. They take life as it comes. Next year meets them as last year (and the year before, and the year before that) left them. They lack vision, purpose and a sense of destiny.

My intent is to challenge such people. I want to awaken in their minds — and confirm in those already so inclined — a sense of our reason for being here on planet earth and for us to seek to fulfill God's purpose for our creation. The God who made us has a plan for us and led by His Spirit, we would be happiest in fulfilling the Master's plan. Of course, we are free moral agents. Unlike the mechanical and electronic systems in our cars that are programmed to work in definite ways, we can choose to fulfill the Designer's plan, or not. My conviction is that we are better off following His plan, for He alone knows the future. I have come to trust the GPS, Waze. Waze can assess the road conditions up ahead and guide me on routes to help me get to my destination faster. I have ignored Waze at times, but only to my own peril. God's plan for my life is like my Waze. I prayerfully seek His wisdom daily and I seek to follow as His Word and His Spirit leads.

God's plan for man is revealed in the Bible, God's love letter to us. Thus, the Bible is cited throughout this book as the basis for ascertaining God's revealed will. To appreciate this book, therefore, it is expected that the reader has made a Christian profession and has accepted the Bible as the Word of God and the rule of faith and practice. Those who do not share this Biblical worldview may also find this work helpful for critically analyzing this description of the Christian lifestyle.

What, then, are the elements of God's plan for our lives? It is a four-part symphony. We are here to **live** as His Word dictates, **love** as He loves, **learn** daily from nature and revelation in interaction with inspired minds, and **look** ultimately for the glorious appearing of the return of Jesus in the clouds of heaven. This final epochal event symbolizes the end of time, as we know it, and the beginning of eternity.

To live, to love, to learn and to look have therefore been used as the four sections of this book. In every section, I developed the concept in four chapters. The chapters are actual adaptations of sermons preached in various congregations over the years. They sum up the kind of information, encouragement and counsel I gave to Tessa, Angelica, thousands of other people, young and old, single and married, as well as counsel I am sharing with you now. My goal has always been to guide others on this exciting journey of growing faith, personal and professional fulfillment, and spiritual empowerment.

It is my hope that every reader would pause to reflect on life's all-important question, which is the theme of this book: "Why are you here?" Please take an introspective look at your life's journey and determine whether your walk thus far has been divinely led, a blessing to others and a benefit to yourself. Have you been living, loving, learning and looking like the Master planned? For those whose self-analysis yields a satisfactory response, I say, journey on in the Lord.

On the other hand, for those whose searching inquiries produce disenchantment with the status quo, I say to you, do not be disillusioned. You may recognize that changes are necessary to effect the desired objectives, but I point you to a God through whom all things are possible. That which now seems so impossible could become a reality through His grace and enabling power. Your best days can be yet ahead! As the songwriter wrote: *It is no secret what God can do. What He has done for others, He can do for you* (Gaither, "It Is No Secret–Bill Gaither.")

None, therefore, need to remain in the frustrating lowlands of personal gloom in life and relationships. Through the grace of God, we all can arise and become what God wants us to be. We can live to be pleased with our response to that searching question, *Why are you here?* for "Christ gives me the strength to face anything," (Philippians 4: 13).

Section One
TO LIVE

He gives us the power to live, and move, and to be who we are
Acts 17:28.

I n this first section of what I choose to call a four-part literary symphony, I provide a word map of the Christian's lifestyle. The profile answers the theme, *"Why are you here?"* by advocating that the Christian is here for worship, fellowship and mission in terms of advancing the kingdom of God. His/her personal goals and life's aspirations are subsumed under this larger objective. This tripartite focus flows from a living faith in God and is evidenced in Christian service to one's fellow man. I conclude the section by pointing out that one can only live for God and fulfill His purpose in life if one has entered partnership or a stewardship relationship with Him. *You cannot do anything without me* (John 15:5).

CHAPTER ONE

Why Are You Here?

This question is actually extracted from the Bible. It was addressed to a dynamic and evangelistic church leader named Elijah. He was a brave, fearless leader for God. He stood against the 450 false prophets at Mount Carmel, and in vintage style uplifted the name and power of Almighty God. The false prophets were thoroughly confounded, and their credibility and their lives destroyed. Elijah was riding the crest wave of spiritual success. He was living as God desired.

Wicked Jezebel had other plans, however. As the devil incarnate, this wicked and adulterous woman decided that she was going to destroy Elijah, for she did not appreciate his standing for what was right, and so Elijah had to run for his life. The angels first caught him under a juniper tree in a terribly frightened state. He was supplied with some food and ran like crazy until we find him in 1 Kings 19 at the entrance of a cave. Here, the Word of the Lord came to him in verse 9: "Why are you here, Elijah?"

What are you doing here? Where's your focus? What brings meaning and purpose to your day? What's your life mission? Why are you here in this pitiable condition? Who's your God?

Isn't He the same God that worked miracles on Mount Carmel? Has He suddenly lost His power to deliver and to save? How can you lose your way because of one sinful woman?

Elijah responded to the Word of the Lord with a litany of woes. He said in verse 10 that he had been jealous for the Lord, but the children of Israel had forsaken the covenant, thrown down the altars and slain the prophets. "I am the only one left and they seek my life." Poor Elijah! You can hear his modern counterparts saying today: "The church is split, sin is rampant, they have run the pastor out of town and I am the only one left!"

It must have pained the heart of God to listen to this diatribe from Elijah. This man of tremendous exploits for God was now bellyaching in a cave, scared to death. Depression is a terrible affliction and it could happen to any of us. The moment we lose our hold on the Lord; the moment we feel that it is *all of me and none of Christ*, we immediately become the target for the enemy. Faith gives way to fear, courage gives way to cowardice, and daring gives way to depression. This was Elijah's predicament at the entrance of the cave. Here was a Christian who didn't know whether he was coming or going. He didn't have a plan for tomorrow. He was simply occupying the ground, waiting for the inevitable! This may sound strangely familiar to many Christians today and, indeed, to many Christian congregations. *Why are you here, Elijah?*

Our loving Lord chose to give Elijah another glimpse of the power of God. Elijah needed to be reminded that he served not mere mortality, but the Mighty God of heaven and earth — the God who rules the elements by the Word of His power. So, God caused a mighty wind to pass by that was so powerful that it broke in pieces the rocks on the mountain. Then the Lord disturbed the earth's foundations and raised up an earthquake.

This was swiftly followed by a great fire. Then the Lord spoke in a still, small voice. Elijah witnessed all of this and then was taken back to the cave where the Word of the Lord came again to him. *Why are you here, Elijah?*

One would have expected that the fresh glimpses of the glory of God would have stirred faith in Elijah and put him back on track with God's plan for his life. This was not a new member in the church. This was a Christian leader of great experience, yet he had drifted so far from God that even fresh revelations of His power did not move him. When we lose our spiritual connections, God's blessings are taken for granted or regarded just as chance occurrences. There is a danger, even today, that experienced Christian leaders get so used to dealing with the business of the church that they lose their spiritual eyesight. When we should be standing in church, giving testimonies and singing that the Lord is blessing me right now, we say, "I was lucky; it just happened that way." But nothing just happens! Our God, the Master of oceans and seas and skies, is always on the job!

To Elijah, the visitation of God made no difference. When asked the same question again, he gave the identical response as before. It seems as if Elijah was programmed to respond in this way. I have visited many churches and have come into contact with many Christians who seem to operate in a pre-programmed way. Their responses are not based on a living relationship with the Lord, but rather on a learned, traditional response. Our conduct at church services, our insipid testimonies and our ineffectual prayers betray the absence of a living relationship with the Lord and descend into mere lip service. Elijah's experience here is a classic case of form replacing faith, religiosity replacing right doing, and the work of God blurring out the God of the work. Get out of your religious rut, Brother and Sister Elijah today, and reflect on this important question: Why are you here?

Elijah was challenged to get back on track in the work of the Lord. Faith is developed through exercise. Social scientists tell us that behaviors influence beliefs. Thus, the Lord sought to resurrect Elijah's faith by getting him involved in the divine enterprise. Go back to your first love; go back to your memorable faith experiences; go back to witnessing and doing exploits for God, for you only develop as a swimmer by swimming! Come out of your cave and get on with your life in harmony with God's will.

The question posed to Elijah is one that can be posed to Christians and Christian congregations today. Like Elijah, I find many Christians and Christian congregations today are in battle-weary mode. Many are sitting under figurative juniper trees and in caves, sullenly saying: "I only am left!" For many, faith is absent, witnessing is non-existent, lives are purposeless, brotherly love is unknown and many are either dead spiritually or just waiting to die. In such churches, traditions are the order of the day; pomp and ceremony abound, but life-giving power is absent. They retain the routine, but there is no life or purpose within.

I remember being invited to speak at a distant country church one day. Our two children, my wife and I arrived at the entrance, and we were immediately taken aback by the huge, four-inch-thick, closed, wooden, double doors that shot up over ten feet before us. This was our first visit to this church on a cold, English winter morning, and we did not know what to expect. We gingerly opened the doors and breathed a sigh of relief as we entered the foyer area. There was no one in the foyer, but ahead of us was another pair of wooden doors — again quite imposing — which led to the main sanctuary. Again, we summoned the courage to push open the doors and saw two groups of worshippers sitting in circles, studying the Bible lesson for that morning. We slipped into the back of one of the classes, nodding a greeting to the one leading as we did so. There was no response or acknowledgment of our presence for the duration of the discussion, which lasted another twenty-five minutes.

As visitors to the church we were not welcomed, offered a hymnal or given any gesture of appreciation for our presence. The first words from anyone to us came at the end of the break period, when the local leader came up to me and inquired if I was the preacher for the day! When I indicated that I was, I was solemnly asked to follow him. Throughout the morning service, I felt a distinct impression that this church was dead set on maintaining its services, but it was mere form and tradition! These poor believers meant well, but Jesus could have entered that church service, and they would not have known it! Why are you here, church?

Neither churches nor individuals must be like that congregation. We are here, first and foremost, to live purposefully and as God intended. To live thus, we must have a connection with God. In *Acts 2,* we have an example of another congregation that was focused on its reason for being. Here were people who knew what they ought to be doing and went about their Father's business.

I want to highlight three salient features of this New Testament congregation as a model for the refocusing and revitalizing of purposeless individuals and churches today. I firmly believe that if we are to live to fulfill God's plans for us, then we must be connected to Him and the rest of His creation through worship and fellowship and have a clear sense of our mission for being here.

WORSHIP

Acts 2:41 recounts the establishment of this New Testament church with the addition of 3,000 souls. We immediately notice that their worship life was something special. In verse 42, they are continuing steadfastly in the apostles' doctrine (Bible study) and in prayers; in verse 46, they are continuing daily in the temple and from house to house, and verse 47 tells us that they are praising God.

Clearly, this church took its worship life seriously. There was no compromise with sin and/or sinners. You can't give light if you are not shining. Sometimes to be politically correct, actions that need to be taken to preserve the standards of the church are not taken and the church is weakened as a result. At the same time, however, the atmosphere of the church did not seem to be cold, ritualistic, or draconian. No! The atmosphere was one of love and prayer and praise.

Every Christian also should be a praise tabernacle. Our lives ought to radiate the glow of heaven. There are some people you dare not ask how they are doing? Their lives are so full of moaning and groaning that they would immediately subject you to a diatribe of woes and injustices done to them that leaves you feeling jaded and downcast. We must learn to praise God anyhow! In the good times praise His Name; at other times, do the same: in everything give thanks for this is the will of God for us.

We know that God is always at work
for the good of everyone who loves him (Romans 8: 28).

The psalmist says: *As long as I can remember, good people have never been left helpless, and their children have never gone begging for food* (Psalm 37:25).

Again, in Psalm 84:11, the psalmist David assures us that God treats us *with kindness and with honor, never denying any good thing to those who live right.*

Instead of moaning and groaning to others who cannot help us, we need to experience the power of prayer. Prayer is the opening of the heart to God as to a friend. The key difference is that God *can* help us. We need to talk less of our woes and pray more concerning them. Sometimes we are more trusting of technology, human expertise, and our well-laid plans than on the power of God. We run the risk of utter dismay and total discouragement if we seek to live our lives apart from the will and power of God. To keep smiling in the sunshine or the storm of life, Christ must be the Lord at the center and circumference of all our plans.

Threats to Our Corporate Worship Today

No Private Devotional Life. There are two major threats to our corporate worship experience. The first is no private devotional life. Too many of us are so busy today that we can find little or no time to maintain a personal walk with God. The stresses of raising a family, holding down two jobs, planning for vacations, and so forth crowd God out of our reckoning. For many, church is a filling station where they come for a quick fill-up for the week. They attend infrequently, frequently late, and leave as early as possible because their agendas are so crowded. This is like the young man who placed a standard prayer at his bedside and said to the Lord nightly as he slouched into bed: "Same as usual, Lord!"

There was a time when Christians really studied their Bibles and took pride in committing large portions of Scripture to memory. This was beneficial not only spiritually, but also academically, for much is now talked about in educational circles about the values of memorization. The spiritually dead in church now want the preachers to do for them what they failed to do throughout the week. As a result, many find church to be boring, and thus they stay away. For them, church becomes a needless routine, a disposable extra that can be dispensed with for any reason — or none. How can you live for God if you do not hear from Him through prayer, study and worship?

The place where dead people congregate is a cemetery, and many churches have become nothing but spiritual cemeteries. It takes a bundle of live coals to make a fire. Thus, when individual members are walking with Christ during the week, they come burning with testimonies to share and their singing and their worshiping give evidence that they serve a risen Savior. A meaningful worship service results from the celebratory coming together of happy, joyous, spiritually alive people who have lived with and for their Lord during the past week. Why are you here? Well, I am here to praise the Lord! As the sun was made to shine, I was made to reflect the glory of the Son of Righteousness!

No Corporate Vision. Routine church activities need to be injected with new life from time to time. The absence of planning means that we do this year just as we did last year, or the year before, or ten years ago, or even fifty years ago! The church must continue to assess its programs and practices for continuing relevance. Yesterday's ways, yesterday's methods, yesterday's people and yesterday's ideas may not be relevant for the challenges of today's problems and people. While core principles and values do not change, practices and policies need to, if the church is to remain relevant and contextual in a changing society. From a critical analysis of the status quo, let us move to adjust the routine, disturb the beleaguered format and remain open and responsive to the Spirit's leading. Also, we need to focus more on engagement of all demographics in the church. If folks are given a piece of the pie, they might just stay on for dinner!

I was in the meeting room of a church one morning, preparing for the worship service. There were five local leaders in attendance, in the absence of the resident pastor. The head elder, seeking to engage in some light conversation, made it known to me that they were all very experienced leaders in that church. He referred to four of them who had all served for over thirty years. Looking at the drab surroundings and the dullness of the earlier service, I mentally noted that their leadership might be a contributing factor, for it is well-known that an organization reflects the spirit of its leaders. The head elder did not refer to the fifth leader that was there, and so I pressed him as to how long this elder had served. "Oh!" he remarked, almost disdainfully, "he just came. He has only served about twelve years!" In that congregation, I saw many who just sat and listened to the service like deified mummies, apparently going through the motions of a religious rite that had little or no relevance to their real lives outside.

What cripples us in maintaining the status quo is, of course, the fear of change. These elders had always been the leaders and, by inference, would always be the leaders. "We have always done it this way," are said to be the seven last words of the church. It is intended to end all discussion and quiet any change agent. However, if worship is to be meaningful, then it must arise out of the current experiences of the members as they live out their Christianity through the week. It's not my brother or my sister, but it's me, O Lord, standing in the need of prayer! It's not a Daniel or a Joseph or an Elijah, but it's me, O Lord, standing in the need of prayer! While I am a strong advocate of order and decency, I am also keenly aware that worship is my offering of praise and should spring from my journey with the Lord.

In a corporate sense, we need to be planning for relevance within our church community. How can we make this church relevant to the needs within a university context, to a farming community, to urban youth and young adults, to those with alternative lifestyles – "my house shall be called a place of worship for all nations," says the Lord in Mark 11:17.

A CNN report highlighted Pastor Ontay Johnson and his wife Gina, who received the news that their child came out as a transgender woman, Kiah Johnson. It was a difficult challenge for the family, but Pastor Johnson came to recognize that he had to let love lead. He was now challenged to continue to love and minister to Kiah. This new reality has been a difficult adjustment for the family, but they continue to live and love as Jesus would. Loving people unconditionally does not mean condoning every detail of their lives. I make no apologies for subscribing to the Biblical worldview on gender identity and encouraging others to live in harmony with the revealed Word of God as outlined in the Scriptures. But I believe that this is best accomplished when I model the lifestyle I am advocating, when I lead with love, and when I recognize the reality of other perspectives. I trust the Holy Spirit to do the rest.

FELLOWSHIP

In Acts 2, we also learn that the church members were rich in fellowship. Verse 42 tells us that they continued in fellowship; verse 44 tells us that they were together and had all things common. Modern churches have gone a long way from this New Testament model. There were over 3,000 people from different languages, cultures and backgrounds, yet they were all together in fellowship.

It may be easier for people to be together in worship. Every five years my religious organization, the Seventh-day Adventists, have over 50,000 members and visitors gathered from around the world in a major city stadium for the worship services of the General Conference. But to reproduce this kind of New Testament fellowship is a much bigger hill to climb. In Christian congregations, many find that it is possible to worship with people, and yet they may have no desire to fellowship with them. The New Testament model challenges us to cease our snobbish indifference and, irrespective of our myriad differences, see others as children of God, and thus our brothers or sisters.

International singing evangelist and my seminarian colleague, Wintley Phipps, tells the following story. After one of his breathtaking performances before a large audience in a major U.S. city, a dear old lady, so enraptured by his musical acumen, rushed up to him and blurted out: "Pastor Phipps, you blessed my heart! When I get to heaven, I must come over to the Black section to hear you sing!"

The New Testament church was united in fellowship! This ugly specter of racism that still blights us and divides us as Christians will not be present in heaven. Despite sermons, sensitivity awareness training and major summits, we still have a long way to go to begin living as God intends — seeing every man or woman as a precious fellow human being for whom Christ died. The language of division and hate that is freely spewed out in our political culture also fuels distance among various demographics, even making us see the other as the enemy.

Divinely-led church leaders have a critical role to play in helping our communities to rediscover the church's role in promoting a caring community. The church is a place of acceptance and affirmation — a therapeutic community that heals the hurts from a godless world. Bruised, battered and buffeted by all the ills that daily afflict us, the church has a role to help adherents enter its fellowship and feel at home — at one with God and at one with the brothers and sisters. Regrettably, there are devilish influences in some churches that continue the blistering, hurting experiences and thus provide no relief from the pains engendered from living during the week in a cold and uncaring world.

I will never forget the Couva Seventh-day Adventist Church in Trinidad, West Indies. When I became a Christian at the age of sixteen, I joined that church fellowship. The members rallied to my support and helped me to grow, not only spiritually but physically as well. I had so many dinner invitations that I needed an organizer to keep up with all my engagements

Enter Agatha Williams. I can't remember why I missed the church services that week, but after the service the following week, Sister Williams approached me and inquired as to the reason for my absence the previous week. I didn't have a good reason and so I lied. "I had no money for the bus fare," I said. I thought that should satisfy her and she would walk away. Well, she didn't. Instead, she went into her huge bag that seemed to carry much of her earthly possessions. Out came two one-dollar notes. "Take that for your bus fare for next week," she said as she tucked the notes into my hand. I placed the notes in my pocket with guilt running all through my veins, for I knew that I got the money under false pretenses.

The worst was yet to come! For several months afterwards, after every church service, Sister Williams would find me without fail, greet me with a smile and a warm handclasp while she placed the two dollars in my hand for my next week's bus fare. I tried to evade her several times, but she was better than a defense missile — she always found her target!

MISSION

The members in that New Testament church enjoyed their walk with God and kept an open-door policy for new believers. Visitors were welcomed. Verse 47 tells us that the Lord added to the church daily those who were being saved. Is your church a welcoming place? If not, what needs to change to let everyone know that they are valued in your congregation?

Sometimes, quite unintentionally, we become so involved in the routine that we neglect the strangers in our midst. Are they comfortably seated? Do they have a program bulletin, or Bible? Do they have a place for dinner after the service? As the visiting worship speaker on many occasions, my wife and I have had to figure out our own meal plans, as there were no hospitality arrangements made for the preacher at the close of the service.

What I particularly see from the New Testament church was that the preaching and teaching were congruent with their living. What they preached, they lived and what they lived, they preached. It's a joy to meet that kind of authentic Christian today. Then, as now, such lives have great power for others to see Christ lifted, not in ostentation or self-aggrandizement, but in humility and love. That which they saw and heard, and that which they personally experienced, they declared to others. Such living and such witnessing have amazing power!

The Bible reminds us that God is not willing that any should perish, but that all should come to repentance. God wants all to be saved, for all are precious in His sight. The Christian message is a global message and every Christian, and every Christian congregation, is a growth cell for the Kingdom. By our lives and by our witness, we are to call men and women from sin unto holiness; from death unto life; and from a hopeless end to endless hope in Christ. That's why we are here! Acts 2, therefore, provides the universal response for congregations and individuals in answer to life's most fundamental question for the Christian: Why are you here?

The Christian, individually and corporately, is here on planet earth to be involved in worship, fellowship and mission *up-reach, in-reach and outreach.* All life emanates from God, and we are to be constantly reaching up to Him through prayer and devotion; to pause to listen to His Spirit talking to us and guiding us through the shoals of life. The need to develop and nurture positive and wholesome relationships with fellow participants of the faith community poses the in-reach challenge. Finally, the call to make disciples of all men, introducing them to Christ and encouraging them by precept and example to live in harmony with the Christian lifestyle is our underpinning mission through all our life's activities. *This is why we are here.*

CHAPTER TWO

Living by Faith

It was a great camp meeting. The rustic scenery from this mountainside retreat was absolutely superb. There was a large crowd present, but there were no distractions during this evangelistic service. The preacher was none other than our Lord Himself. The Word was being proclaimed with mighty power. The sick was being healed, lives were being transformed, and people everywhere were just rejoicing and praising the Name of the Lord.

As His colleagues in ministry, Jesus' disciples were delighted at this great spiritual awakening. As far as they could see, it was a marvelous convocation. In this wonderful spirit of inspiration and praise, none seemed to have noticed that the time had literally flown by, and the sun was now setting along the western horizon.

Gradually however, the reality of the lateness of the hour dawned on the disciples. As the meeting wore on, they began to sense that there would be a problem in finding food to feed such a vast multitude that would doubtless be very hungry after such a long day. Finally, the disciples went to the side and convened a committee meeting.

The one item on the agenda was the feeding of this vast throng, estimated at over 12,000, including women and children. The committee reasoned that there were no food outlets in the immediate vicinity and the treasurer must have indicated that even if there were, no funds in the budget were available to cover this expense. After all, there couldn't have been since Judas, the treasurer, used to help himself to money from the bag. The disciples therefore reported their decision to Jesus. Luke 9: 12 records their voted action: ...*Send the crowd to the villages and farms around here. They need to find a place to stay and something to eat. There is nothing in this place. It's like a desert!*

As far as the disciples were concerned, and from a purely human perspective, this action seemed a sensible, logical, and pragmatic one. They had no food and no money, so let the people take care of themselves as best they could. They reasoned that their role was simply to preach to others; how they lived thereafter was none of their concern. These disciples did not see how they could ever supply food for such a large multitude. Have you found yourself in a situation where you thought the situation was just too big for you? You felt overwhelmed by the enormity of the challenge? I have.

While serving as president of the University of the Southern Caribbean, for several months we had serious challenges in meeting our payroll. One month, my administrators and I were on a planning retreat one day before salaries were due when we got word that the tuition check we were depending on from the government was delayed. We turned the planning meeting into a prayer meeting and trusted God to provide once again for His school. We asked our CFO to go in person to the government finance office. Would you believe that, miraculously, she was able to leave that office with a check in her hand that would more than cover the payroll? *The just shall live by faith* (Romans 1:17, KJV).

The disciples were acting purely from the facts. They decided based on what they knew and saw and were able to reason for themselves. However, this approach had a missing dimension: faith. The person living and operating simply by the facts looks only at what is humanly possible, but he who lives by faith looks at the facts, but also, he looks beyond the facts into considering what God can do – in addition to or in spite of the factual reality. It is the thrilling privilege of the Christian to live by faith and not merely by sight. The disciples were guilty of making decisions based purely on the facts of the circumstances, without exercising any faith in what Christ can do.

When we live purely on the facts before us, we can become easily overwhelmed and stressed. We moan that "it can't be done". We opt for easier and more convenient alternatives, even though they are unsatisfactory. We settle for less than the best because that's what the facts suggest. Refusing to extend our vision by faith to reach out to that which seems to be beyond our reach is to limit the Almighty God that we serve. Living purely on the gruesome facts of a situation demonstrates a failure to recognize that you are not alone on this big earth and that you have a Heavenly Father who desires you to succeed. He is willing to give you more than you can think, or ask, or even desire, if you can only trust Him by faith. His presence and power are there for you.

Living purely on the facts is to live apart from God. Therefore, you make decisions purely on the merits or demerits of a particular case. However, such an approach stymies your best performance, frustrates in the achievement of your desired goals and may even prevent you from fulfilling your life's mission.

The facts could imprison you in doubt and fear and leave you feeling helpless and inadequate.

Elijah moved from faith to facts as he went from Mount Carmel to the cave. In the former case, he looked beyond the visible to what God can do while in the latter, he was so filled with fear that he could not even appreciate that it was the messenger of God talking to him. Thus, he had no adequate answer to the question: Why are you here? The apostle Peter was walking on water by faith, but the facts took over, and he began to drown. Elijah's and Peter's experiences are repeated by many today and they justify their stance by claiming that they are being realistic. In reality, they doubt God's ability to work in their situation.

There are some people who are confirmed pessimists. The story is told of a man who stood at a rail station in the mid western United States in the last century. The locomotive train was making its first journey through his town. The townspeople were very excited, for they were about to witness an historic event. The excitement rose as the train was seen in the distance, making its way into their station for the very first time. Amidst the noise of the people, this doubter could be heard to exclaim that, from what he knows about trains, it could never stop at the station. The train came into the station and, sure enough, it pulled to a stop. You would think that this would have convinced this pessimist. Well, it didn't. He now predicted that this train could never start again. At the appropriate time, however, the train pulled out of the station as it continued its westward journey. As it disappeared into the distance, this confirmed pessimist was heard to exclaim that the train would never stop again!

There are some incurable pessimists, even among us today. Such people limit their potential and possibilities because, for whatever reason, they are always of the view that no matter what the challenge, it just cannot be done! How we forget that we are here to live by faith and thereby glorify our Lord!

Let's get back to the story. I can imagine that the disciples passed a hurried note to Jesus. *You have got to close the meeting and send these people away to buy their food.* Some of the disciples probably even started to grumble that Jesus was preaching too long. After all, why should He keep the people so long out in the desert? Any time there is a problem, we usually find someone else to blame. Blaming the leader for any mishap is a common practice! So, blame Jesus for the problem. Let Him send the people to find a meal wherever they could, and let the church roll on!

There could be a great gap between our profession and our practice as followers of Christ. We proclaim His love in such melodious tones, but when the opportunity comes for us to demonstrate that love, we come up wanting. For instance, we tell others how much God loves them, then we leave them, not pausing to consider whether God wants to use us to meet any of their needs.

Sometimes, even members are hesitant to invite a fellow brother, sister or a family home for dinner for fear that the meal may not be enough or that it may not be good enough. That is living by facts only. I have seen how God multiplies the roast, and the macaroni pie, and the salad, and the drinks to feed so much more than we had anticipated. Why are you here? I am here to live by faith in a mighty, miracle-working God.

Jesus listened to the recommendation of the disciples. Then, he stumped them as Matthew recorded in chapter 14, verse 16, *They don't have to leave. Why don't you give them something to eat?*

This was a fascinating question. In it is combined both a rebuke and a challenge. Jesus saw that these disciples were simply trying to get rid of a problem any way they could, without any consideration whatsoever as to whether these people would really find any food. In short, they were just trying to cover their tracks and Jesus saw through their guile. Thus, His challenge: Don't let them go. You give them something to eat. All God's biddings are enabling. Whatever He asks us to do, He gives us the power to do. Thus, when Jesus asked His disciples to provide for the people, He was thereby guaranteeing their success in this undertaking, for He never leads His people into failure.

I hear someone asking: What do you mean by *God never leads His people into failure?* Look at me. I am a child of God. I serve Him faithfully. Yet I have this terminal illness that is wrecking my body and giving me excruciating pain and anguish. Or look at me, I prayed to the Lord so many times and yet, I failed my examinations. Or, how about me, I love the Lord but yet He took my loved one away from me. How could you say that God does not lead His people into failure? I feel like a failure right now.

I want to suggest that it is all a matter of perspective. The directive of Jesus was simply an invitation to His disciples to move into the faith dimension. Living by faith does not ignore the facts of a situation, but it places a new perspective on them. Faith is not opposed to the known facts but is in addition to them. Faith asks not only what man can do but, more importantly, what God can do in a given situation.

As a young Christian, I remember sitting in the dining room at Caribbean Union College (now University of the Southern Caribbean) the morning after the school chapel was completely destroyed by fire. We were singing praises to the Lord. Then Dr. Bernard Benn, the college president, got up and uttered words I shall never forget. He said: "We Christians are a strange people. We have just had our chapel burned to the ground and here we are, praising the Lord." That's living by faith. When you live by faith, you live with the consciousness that *God is always at work for the good of everyone who loves him* (Romans 8:28).

Do you remember a man named Job? Do you remember how much he lost? If ever there was a Christian who experienced great failures, Job was one. What was his testimony? *God may kill me, but still, I will trust him* (Job 13:15). It's just a matter of perspective. From a human standpoint, our life situation may look like a failure. However, when the spotlight of faith focuses on it, then we will see a thousand reasons why we should praise the Lord.

Let me share a personal experience. After serving for some years as a minister and an educator in the Caribbean, I was granted study leave by my employers to pursue a doctorate in Michigan. My wife, Martha, and our children (Clintelle and Clinson) all moved with me to Michigan where we lived for the duration of my study. My wife also pursued graduate studies. I finished my program on schedule and was prepared to return to the Caribbean. Our permanent home was there, all our relatives were there, and all our future career aspirations were tied up with the Caribbean, as far as we were concerned. I duly informed my employers that I was through with my studies and was therefore ready to return home.

For various reasons, it became clear that my employers felt that my services were no longer desired. This was a bitter pill to swallow. I was in student housing with a family to feed, huge bills to pay and with no money and no employment. I felt discouraged, depressed and a total failure. As a family, we were shattered. My wife couldn't study and flunked her comprehensive examination. Nevertheless, we kept together in prayer. I remember preparing a sermon at that time which I entitled, "In God's Waiting Room!"

Quite unexpectedly, an invitation came for us to work in Britain. My wife actually took the call from Pastor Cecil Perry, then the president of the South England Conference. The plans moved rapidly and within a few months, we were on a flight to London and the commencement of an exciting new phase of our lives. Upon reflection, we thanked God for disappointing us on the return to the Caribbean, for if we had a choice between the Caribbean and England, we would have opted to go where we knew and had well-established roots. We would thus have missed out on a valuable opportunity for service in Europe.

Listen to the words of an inspired Christian author:

> *"God never leads His children otherwise than they would choose to be led, if they could see the end from the beginning, and discern the glory of the purpose which they are fulfilling as coworkers with Him," Desire of Ages, pp.224-225.*

Helen Keller was born deaf and blind, yet she painstakingly developed her powers of speech, graduated from college, and conducted world lecture tours on behalf of the deaf and the blind. She wrote several books before her death, which occurred less than a generation ago. Was she a failure because of her disabilities? Certainly not!

From a human standpoint, you may be in a failing situation, but you do not have to be a failure. Our God could turn around your situation anytime as He chooses, or He could give you grace and wisdom to see it as He sees it. Of this I am assured: God wants us to prosper and be in health, even as our soul prospers.

What, then, is living by faith? It is pausing to prayerfully inquire what is the will of God on the issue at hand. It is studying His Word on a regular, systematic basis so that you become more acquainted with Him and His will for you as His follower. It is the willingness to be open-minded and responsive to the leading of His Holy Spirit as He impresses your heart.

Living by faith is unhesitatingly building an ark and preaching for 120 years, even though you have never seen a drop of rain fall from the sky. Living by faith is challenging an uncircumcised Philistine into battle with just your sling and five stones. Living by faith is standing up against hundreds of heathen prophets and proclaiming fearlessly that the Lord, He is God. Living by faith is believing without seeing, trusting without knowing, following without fully understanding. It is acknowledging that God says it, I believe it, and that settles it.

Living by faith is seeing the Red Sea of problems before you yet hearing amidst the din of angry waves the clarion command of your Master to go forward in faith. It is being thrown into a den of hungry lions, yet remaining true and steadfast, knowing that God would either change the situation or change you in the situation. I have heard so many testimonies of believers who have glorified God for their afflictions, for through these we learn the way of the Cross. Through trials, we triumph gloriously.

Yes, Jesus challenged His disciples to live by faith. That's why we are here and that's the glorious way He expects Christians to live! How else could Jesus see a crowd of 12,000 hungry people before Him with no food, and no budgetary provision, and yet say to the disciples, "Why don't you give them something to eat"? But then again, if the disciples — as the leaders of the church — couldn't exercise faith in God's power, how could they expect it from the followers? They should have been exhibits of the life of faith.

Thus, on that mountainside retreat, the congregation witnessed faith in action. A humble youngster with five barley loaves and two fishes surrendered all that he had to Jesus. I praise the Lord for him. If we would give our all to the Master, what miracles could be wrought! What lives could be blessed! Isn't it a joy to know that the Lord could take my poor, humble gift and use it to bless a multitude? Somebody could be blessed by what you have if you turn it over to Jesus.

Jesus blessed the meal, broke it, and passed it on to his disciples, who passed it on to the waiting congregation. He blessed and broke and passed; blessed and broke and passed; until everyone was fed, and twelve baskets were left over.

Interestingly, these faithless leaders had now become the channels of blessing. The same men who had tried to get out of the problem were now part of the solution! Thank God, He never casts us off because of our lack of faith. He gives us all another chance. He gently encourages us to come up higher, to increase our faith in Him. I encourage you right now to offer this simple prayer: Lord, increase my faith in You so that I would trust You even when I cannot trace You.

The faith of the multitude must have been strengthened by this miraculous sight in the desert. More importantly, I believe that the disciples learned a great lesson. They learned that there is no emergency with God. They learned that there is nothing too hard for Him to do. They saw that man's extremity was but God's opportunity; man's miraculous was but God's routine. They saw a God who is able to do so much more than they could ever think or ask or desire; a God in whom all things are possible.

Why Are You Here?

One day, a nine-year old girl was on a transatlantic flight when the plane ran into some terrible weather conditions. The plane started to tilt from side to side and objects began to fall off from the compartments above and from the serving areas. The elderly gentleman sitting next to the girl was very scared and began to pray aloud. This girl was not in the least bit scared. She was singing merrily and playing with her doll as if everything was absolutely fine.

Finally, the elderly gentleman couldn't stand it anymore and he called out to her. "Little girl, we could die, you know. Aren't you afraid?"

The little girl smiled happily and said, "No, I am not afraid!"

"Why aren't you afraid?" insisted the scared gentleman.

"Because my daddy is the pilot," she responded.

Isn't it reassuring to know that, as we go through our challenges in life, our Daddy is the pilot? No matter what the situation, we may go forward in faith for ultimate victory. Like Job we can say:

I know that my Protector lives, and at the end he will stand on this earth. My flesh may be destroyed, yet from this body I will see God. Yes, I will see him for myself, and I long for that moment (Job 19:25-27).

Dear reader, we have been created to live by faith in a mighty God with whom all things are possible! You are, therefore, to constantly challenge the facts in every situation before you in the light of the Word and will of God. Ask yourself, *how is my faith in God leading me to act in this situation?* This is not a call to live presumptuously, but to live by faith, for it is faith that is built on the promises of God. Living by faith is a solemn recognition that God can and still does work on behalf of His children. It is the best way to live, and trust me, it's so exciting! Living by faith is what we ought to be doing here. *The just shall live by faith* (Romans 1:17, KJV).

CHAPTER THREE

Religion in Working Clothes

How does living by faith translate into our everyday lives? How does it move from some kind of intangible concept in the sky to something down-to-earth and practical? How do we put this faith religion into working clothes for everyday wear? The story in Luke 10 provides us with some answers.

In Luke 10:25, we find Jesus resting with His disciples when a learned Jewish scholar approaches Him with a fundamental question: "What must I do to inherit eternal life?" Knowing his legal training, Jesus pointed the inquirer back to the law. This requires one to love the Lord with all one's heart and your neighbor as yourself. The lawyer had no difficulty with the first part but wanted clarification. "Who is my neighbor?" he questioned. In response, Jesus proceeded to set forth three perspectives on dealing with your neighbors, three ways of identifying and responding to those around you who are in need, three ways of putting your faith and religion into practice. First, let us go back in time and recapture the scene that Jesus portrayed for this student of the law.

A traveler was on a journey from Jerusalem down to Jericho when he was robbed, beaten, and left half-dead, lying along the pass. Note that Jesus did not spend a moment to describe who the traveler was. Not a word was said about his rank, his descent, or his religion. He could have been a rich man, poor man, beggar-man, or thief, it did not matter. He could have been Jew, Gentile, or Greek; English, Irish or black; West Indian or American, it did not matter. The only important issue was that he was a human being — a person with flesh and blood; a person with feelings and emotions; a person who could cry and laugh; a person who could feel hurt and rejection; a person who could love and be loved. That was the only important thing as far as Jesus was concerned.

I am often asked the question, "Where are you from?" Most of the time the question is asked with the best of intentions, the individual genuinely wanting to get better acquainted. Sometimes also, my particular accent confuses people. I have been thought to be Barbadian, Guyanese, African-American, and Trinidadian. It has happened, however, that a person's reaction to me has significantly changed when I inform them of my country of origin. Somehow, it didn't meet their expectations. It is wrong to regard people differently simply because of something they had no control over, such as their place of birth. We should not judge people by any external factors, such as the country of their origin, the color of their skin, the texture of their hair, or even the size of their bank account. We all know what an evil prejudice is, and as followers of Christ we must work to eliminate, not perpetuate it.

As we return to the story in Luke 10, we see that the journey to Jericho was a dangerous one. It was a distance of about twenty miles, and it entailed a descent of almost 3,500 feet through a portion of the dry, barren, uninhabited hills of the wilderness of Judah. This roadway had been the haunt of thieves and desperadoes and became known as "The Way of Blood". The entire region, with its many caves and rocks, provided a perfect hideout for robbers.

Thus, we can all picture the scene. An injured man lying helplessly on the roadside, obviously in need of some help from a fellow human being. Now Jesus went on to present the three attitudes adopted by people in dealing with neighbors in need. These three ways were portrayed by three characters: a priest, a Levite, and a Samaritan. One was a religious leader, the other a lay associate, and the third a foreigner to the Jews. The likely nationality of the injured traveler was Jewish.

The Attitude of the Priest

The first attitude towards neighbors was demonstrated by the priest. The Bible records that when the priest saw the injured man, he passed by on the other side. In short, the priest was not interested. He felt that it had nothing to do with him. Interestingly, this priest must have been on his way either to or from the religious services at the temple in Jerusalem. He was a religious man, a man known for his holiness, but he passed by on the other side. He saw no connection between what he preached in the temple and what he practiced on the street; no connection between loving God and loving his neighbor; no connection between sanctity and charity.

I am sure, reader, that you understand what I am saying, for I am not talking about some strange, foreign stuff to Christians. I am sure we know people (possibly even ourselves) who are very good at reciting texts, giving testimonies, being first at church, and even give talks on helping our fellow men, and yet they won't spare a dime even if a life depends on it. Like the lawyer who came to Jesus, many find that serving God is the easy part. The real test is loving our neighbors. This is the challenge: to bring our religion out of the holy cloister and make it an everyday, working-clothes one.

We must also enlarge the concept of helping our neighbors beyond the realm of mere physical help. The people around us are languishing for the want of knowledge of Christ, His Christocentric value system as described in His Word, and His soon return in the clouds of glory. We talk to our associates about politics, business, sports, and the current economic problems; but do we introduce them to the most important person in our lives — Jesus Christ? Or do we, like the priest, say, *I am not interested in helping my neighbor here? I just don't have the time or the will to help.*

Here's a statement from Ellen White, my favorite Christian author, that has stayed with me over the years:

> We should never forget that we are placed on trial in this world, to determine our fitness for the future life. None can enter heaven whose characters are defiled by the foul blot of selfishness. Therefore, God tests us here, by committing to us temporal possessions, that our use of these may show whether we can be entrusted with eternal riches (Counsels on Stewardship).

It is our Christian duty to use the resources God has entrusted to us to bless the lives of those who come within our sphere of influence. That's why we are here.

The Attitude of the Levite

Let us look at another way of relating to our neighbors, as demonstrated by the Levite. The Scriptures tell us in *Luke 10:32* that the Levite came over and looked at the helpless traveler and then went on his way. The Levite was interested in the problem but didn't want to get involved. His attitude was that somebody else would help this unfortunate man.

He is the type who will sit in his rocking chair and complain about the ills of society but won't lift a finger to help. He wouldn't volunteer his time, his talents, or his resources. He is never able to give money for any project, to spend time in any volunteer activity, or reach out to those who are hurting around him. He is only interested in talking about the problem, but not in doing anything about it.

The truth is that if you ever hear people like the priest and Levite talk, you will feel that they are ready for Heaven. They sound so pious, so holy but they are so heavenly-minded they are no earthly good. Much of it is mere pretense. The Bible says in 1 John 4:20: *"But if we say we love God and don't love each other, we are liars. We cannot see God. So how can we love God if we don't love the people we can see?*

I remember hearing my good friend — Pastor Walter Pearson, now deceased — tell the story about the time he and his wife went to buy a house. When they looked into the back garden, they saw a tall tree all laden with strawberries. For a moment, it looked quite tempting to see all those strawberries just waiting to be picked and eaten. Then he remembered: strawberries do not grow on tall trees like that. He, therefore, went close by to investigate further. A good thing he did, for he found that some prankster had decided to hang plastic strawberries all over the tree. It was all pretense. Some Christians are like that. They hang an aura of holiness all over them, but it is not real; it is all deception. Why are you here? I am here to live that kind of faith religion that is evident in my everyday dealings with my fellow men. My faith mantra is: what would Jesus do (WWJD) in this situation?

The Attitude of the Samaritan

The third approach to dealing with a neighbor was seen in the example of the Samaritan. His was not a religion of forms and ceremonies, but what I choose to describe as a working clothes religion. He had a simple motto for his life: when you see good to do, just do it! Thus, he took care of the stranger, bound his wounds, took him to an inn, and left an open check to pay for the expenses of the injured man until he was well again. This Samaritan risked his own safety to come to the help of a man who normally would have hated him, for Jews hated the Samaritans. That did not matter. Here was a man in need; he was, therefore, a neighbor indeed!

This was a real, working clothes religion: the religion of love. It is a love that is not concerned with self, but with service. It is a love that regards every man as a brother, and every woman as a sister. It is a love that treats all with dignity and respect, whatever their social class or economic status. It is a love that breaks down barriers and builds bridges to other people. It is a love that makes us willing to get our hands dirty, our cars soiled, our homes inconvenienced, even our reputations endangered in order to help those in need.

Jesus took the love your neighbor message to the ultimate: 'The greatest way to show love for friends is to die for them' (John 15:13).

Also note this statement from the book *Christ Object Lessons*, p. 69: "*Christ is waiting with longing desire for the manifestation of Himself in His church. When the character of Christ shall be perfectly reproduced in His people, then He will* come *to claim them as His own*, ("Christ's Object Lessons.")"

This last quotation summarizes in one simple concept what we have been talking about – the character of Christ. The character of man is, by nature, selfish; the character of Christ, by nature, is unselfish. Man, so loves himself that he keeps. On the other hand, God so loved the world that He gave. We truly belong to Christ, not merely when we profess His name, attend His church, or recite His Word, but when we reflect His character in our everyday lives. When our religion moves from the pews of the church and the prayers in our closets to positively impact the people of the community during the week, then we are fulfilling the purpose for our existence and satisfactorily responding to the question, "Why are you here?"

The parable of the good Samaritan presents us with two kinds of holiness: the spurious and the genuine. The priest and the Levite demonstrated a religion that is merely form and ceremony but is as lifeless as the hills of Gilboa. Such a religion neither satisfies nor saves, for it reaps the same rewards as the openly selfish and unholy. On the other hand, the religion of the Samaritan showed that the God of love and mercy was reigning in his heart. He was a faithful steward using his time, his talents, and his resources to assist another. *Whenever you did it for any of my people, no matter how unimportant they seemed, you did it for me* (Matthew 25:40).

The story is told of a public speaking competition that was being held on Psalm 23. The best orators of the land were on display. There were three finalists. After the first orator did his rendition, there were cheers from the large crowd. After the second finalist did his presentation, there was tumultuous applause and a standing ovation. He was certainly the man to beat.

Then came the turn of the third finalist to render the psalm. He was an old man, and he took his time about it. His presentation was filled with such earnestness, pathos and sensitivity that he held his audience spellbound even after he was through. When he was done, one could have heard the proverbial pin dropping to the floor, so mesmerized and awestruck was the audience. In fact, there were tears in the eyes of many. The old man was asked the reason why his presentation evoked such a different response in his listeners. His answer was simple: "The other finalists knew the psalm, but I know the Good Shepherd." Knowing and following the Good Shepherd in our everyday walk is why we are here!

CHAPTER FOUR

Partnership with God

I have sought thus far to profile the Christian lifestyle in terms of worship, fellowship, mission, faith and service. All of these are derived from a connection, or what I call a partnership, with God. We are reminded in Acts 17:28: *He gives us the power to live, to move, and to be who we are.* A partnership is traditionally seen as a form of business arrangement in which two or more persons are associated in carrying on commercial or professional activities usually sharing the profits and losses in specified proportions. Ordinarily, a partnership involves a 50/50, a 60/40, or 2/3 to 1/3 arrangement. The idea is that both parties contribute to the partnership, and both share the gains or the losses in the agreed ratio of support.

In the partnership with God, however, one party contributes everything while the other provides nothing. Also, this partnership is not a professional or commercial one, but a spiritual one. Again, this partnership is intended to benefit or enrich, not both partners but only one, and it's the one that has contributed nothing. What a partnership! As I develop this fascinating theme, I will focus on:

1. The Partners in the Partnership
2. The Purpose of the Partnership
3. The Product or Result of the Partnership

The Partners in the Partnership

The Chief Partner in this relationship is our Creator, our Owner, our Maker, God Himself. The psalmist exclaims: *The earth and everything in it, including the people, belong to the Lord* (Psalms 24: 1).

The book of Genesis begins with the declarative statement: *In the beginning God created the heavens and the earth* (Genesis 1: 1).

In the book of Revelation, chapter 14 and verse 7, God's people are called back to *Worship and honor God! The time has come for him to judge everyone. Kneel down before the one who created heaven and earth, the oceans, and every stream.*

What these passages of Scripture tell us in no uncertain terms is that everything and everyone belongs to God by creation. All that I am and all that I possess or ever would possess belong to God, for He alone is the Great Owner!

God is, therefore, the Great Partner. He is the One who owns the cattle on a thousand hills, who spoke, and it was done, who commanded, and it stood fast. He is the Great I Am; the Glorious One; the all-knowing One; the all-seeing One.

The other partner in this relationship is, of course, mankind. We are creatures made by God and we came on the stage of action on the sixth day of creation week. When Adam and Eve arrived, everything was already created. They contributed nothing to the creation; indeed, they were products of it. Therefore, they owned nothing. Their lives and all their concomitant blessings were gifts from a loving heavenly Father.

Mystery of mysteries! Despite this, God called man and gave him management over all of God's creation. The psalmist expressed his amazement at this privilege thus:

> *I often think of the heavens your hands have made, and of the moon and stars you put in place. Then I ask, Why do you care about us humans? Why are you concerned for us weaklings? You made us a little lower than you yourself, and you have crowned us with glory and honor. You let us rule everything your hands have made. And you put all of it under our power. (Psalms 8: 3-6)*

At creation, God made our fore parents stewards of their lives and the rest of the earth. They were given positions of trust. Their role was not to be that of mere servants, but that of stewards. Stewards identify with their masters. They act in their master's absence, doing as their master would do were he presiding. The position of a steward is one of dignity, because it signifies the trust of the master.

What a privilege for man to be in partnership with God! What an honor to be entrusted with the management of God's creation! What a joy to have life, and health, and spiritual, mental and physical endowments. Yes, talents, abilities, skills, expertise — all to be developed and managed by us for God as His faithful stewards.

Just imagine! The delicate touch of the physician's hand, her power over nerve and muscle, her knowledge of the delicate organism of the body, are all the wisdom of divine power given to her. The skill with which the carpenter uses the hammer, the wisdom and knowledge needed to send man into space, the mysteries of modern computer technology, are all but demonstrations of God's gifts to the human family. It is such a joy to know that our Heavenly Partner has created and gifted us so that we may satisfactorily fulfill our purpose here.

The Purpose of the Partnership

The big question is: why has God so favored man? What's in it for God? Did God create man as little imps to selfishly enhance His glory? No! A thousand times *no*!

> God is the source of life and light and joy to the universe. Like rays of light from the sun, blessings flow out from him to all the creatures he has made. In his infinite love He has granted men the privilege of becoming partakers of the divine nature, and, in their turn, of diffusing blessings to their fellowmen... Those are brought nearest to their Creator who thus become participants in labors of love... the man who for the sake of selfish indulgence ignores the wants of his fellow men, the miser who heaps up his treasures here,–is withholding from himself the richest blessing that God can give him. ("Counsels on Stewardship," 2023.)

What a glorious concept – to be partakers of the divine nature. Our God wants us to reflect His character in all our dealings and has gifted us so to do. God has endowed every human being with time, talents, physical assets, resources or treasures and a body. These are to be used purposefully and as God desires. We cannot afford to squander any of these gifts or to use them for selfish gain or pleasure. We are to guard these resources as a holy trust for which we will be called upon to give an account.

I still remember the day when I took possession of my E350 Mercedes Benz. It was metallic champagne with tan leather seats, a tan dashboard and mahogany trims. I felt on top of the world to own this vehicle. I was given the manual containing all the instructions for the optimum maintenance of this car. Yes, it was now my car, and I could have chosen to do whatever I wanted with it; but I didn't. I meticulously followed the manufacturer's instructions, for I wanted the best from my car. Although it was a costly undertaking, I maintained the service schedule from the company's agents, used the right grade of gas and quickly attended to any seeming defect. I knew that I would get the best from my car if I faithfully followed the maker's instructions.

It's the same with our lives. The God who made us desires us to live our best lives. Yes, we have the power of choice and so we may choose to ignore His Divine directives and live as we please. I also could have chosen to ignore the manufacturer's instructions and put water in the gas tank and gas in the radiator! However, we gain the most when we do it the maker's way. It is only as we fulfill the divine purpose in our creation that life can be a blessing to us. We are the happiest when we follow the Master's plan.

Therefore, it makes sense to live as God desires, to love even as He loves, and to give even as He gives. Our role in the partnership is to use time wisely and as God intends. We are to maximize our talents and our treasures to be a blessing to others, and to seek to have every thought, every act, every motive pulsates with selfless love for God and man. We can then look forward to finally entering the eternal joys of the redeemed. I guarantee you that this is the best way to live here.

The Product or Result of the Partnership

Eternal life with Jesus is the end result of this partnership. God wants to give us eternal life. He wants us to have bodies that never tire, lives without sickness or pain, a land where no evil dwells, a place to call home forever, and minds that are forever learning!

Just imagine! No prisons, no hospitals, no funerals, no death. What a joy to be constantly in the pink of health and in the sparkle of youth. What a privilege to be able to soar to worlds unknown — forever learning, forever blessed, forever becoming more and more into the image and likeness of our Heavenly Father and Divine Partner.

Listen to the welcoming words of our Lord: *'Wonderful!' his master replied. 'You are a good and faithful servant. I left you in charge of only a little, but now I will put you in charge of much more. Come and share in my happiness!'* (Matthew 25:21). Again, in the same chapter: *My father has blessed you! Come and receive the kingdom that was prepared for you before the world was created* (Matthew 25:34).

Legend has it that a diamond cutter was at work one day, grinding away on a piece of diamond. However, this piece of diamond complained at the grinding he was receiving. He was getting more grinding than all the other pieces around. "Stop grinding me so much," he screamed. "Don't grind me anymore. I am *not* going to take it anymore."

The diamond cutter remained silent amidst all the complaints. Finally, he responded to the piece of diamond, "Do you see that beautiful King's crown on the table over there?" Yes!

"Do you see the small space in the center at the front?" Yes! "Well, that's where I am preparing you for. You are going to be the centerpiece on the King's crown." The diamond couldn't hold back his excitement at such good news. He shouted back to the diamond cutter, "Just keep on grinding until I fit just right!"

Heaven is our home. Eternity is our destiny. Before the triumphs there, however, we have our challenges here. Connected to Him, our Heavenly Partner, we may live for the honor of His name by His grace! We fulfill the purpose of our creation when we regard our bodies, our time, our talents, and our treasures as His holy trust and use them for His glory! That's why we are here!

SECTION TWO
TO LOVE

"God is love, and anyone who does not love others has never known him,"
(1 John 4:8)

In this second section of our four-part literary symphony, I discuss the concept of love in the Christian experience. First, I look at the connection between love and Christian standards from the example of Jesus. I then proceed to provide some counsel and guidance for spouses and singles for managing their emotions and their love relationships. Finally, I elaborate on the loving Christian attributes of appreciation for those who have blessed us and forgiveness for those who have done us wrong. Together, these four chapters provide a gestalt as to how we ought to love here on earth.

CHAPTER FIVE

LOVE MUST BE TOUGH

The tenth chapter of Mark is a journalistic dream. I see headlines such as: "Jesus Makes the Blind See"; "Jesus Settles Team Dispute"; "Jesus Issues Firm Statement On Divorce"; "Jesus Cuddles the Children". Yes, it looks very much as if Jesus was constantly on a winning streak. He was successful, well-liked, and confident. That is, except for verses 17-22 of the chapter. This headline may well read: "Youth Turns His Back On Jesus".

This rich young ruler had great possessions and occupied a position of major responsibility. He had watched Jesus longingly as Jesus cuddled and blessed the children. He felt deeply attracted to Jesus and so he ran to meet Him. In simplicity of heart and genuineness of spirit, he respectfully placed the question on his heart before Jesus: "Good Teacher, what can I do to have eternal life?"

Jesus looked at the young man and loved him. He longed to give him that peace, grace and joy that would transform his life. He longed to see him in His service, spreading the good news of the kingdom. Yes, Jesus loved him and saw tremendous potential in him. This ruler had youth, energy, and enthusiasm going for him, but he lacked one great essential — a commitment to the Lord. Jesus did not occupy first place in his life.

This ruler, therefore, couldn't come to Jesus as he was. There were certain changes that were necessary if this love relationship with his Lord was to thrive. So, Jesus laid down the standards, "Sell what you have and give to the poor, then come and follow Me." Our Lord was merely testing this young man on the vital principle that lies at the basis of any love relationship: you must leave what you have and go after what you want.

There can be no divided loyalties in love. If we want to follow the Lord, we must be fully committed to Him. "Take the whole world but give me Jesus," must be the song of my heart. This was too much for this youth. The Bible tells us that the young man walked away grieved, for he had great possessions. Whether these possessions were his cars, homes, or stocks and bonds, the real issue here was that he placed these ahead of a relationship with His Lord.

Picture the scene with me. There is the anguish on the face of Jesus as He sees one He loves walking away from His presence. This young man is never heard from again in Scripture. Couldn't Jesus lower the standard or run after him, pleading or trying to negotiate with the young man? Couldn't Jesus say, "Come anyhow"? "Maybe you will change later," or "Since you have so much talent, I will wink at your lack of commitment and accept you anyhow"? No! Jesus sets the supreme standard for discipleship and leaves an open door. "Do you love me more than these?" is His simple query. Herein lies the essence of true love. True love does not force or entrap anyone. Rather, it sets the standards and leaves an open door. That's why I affirm with Christian psychologist and author, Dr. James Dobson of *Focus on the Family,* that love must be tough, for it takes a tough love to function in such a principled manner.

In his sample letter for a married person to send to his/her spouse who is requesting divorce, Dr. Dobson wrote:

> ... *I now realize that I have been attempting to hold you against your will. That simply can't be done. As I reflect on our courtship and early years together, I'm reminded that you married me of your own free choice. I did not blackmail you or twist your arm or offered you a bribe. It was a decision you made without pressure from me. Now you say you want out of the marriage, and obviously, I have to let you go. ... You are free to go. If you never call me again, then I will accept your decision.* James Dobson, Love must be Tough, p. 47, (Word Books, 1978/ "Hope for Dying Marriages.").

While Dr. Dobson's book focuses particularly on couples in crisis, his principles of loving toughness are valid for all love relationships. True love is not weak, frail, cheap or beggarly. It does not beg, plead or grovel. It does not throw out the standards and accept another at any cost. It is not governed by feelings, asserting that if it feels good, then you are free to do it. Let me elaborate on three dimensions of this concept of true love.

True Love is Principled

First, true love is principled. There should be no compromising, no winking, and no shifting from principle. Jesus loved the young man dearly, but He just couldn't have him at any price.

That young man still had other loves competing for his highest affections — money, wealth, and possessions — and he had to change his priorities if he were to love Jesus supremely.

This ruler had to make a choice between his savings and his Savior; his jewels and his Jesus; his loves and his Lord. Jesus challenged him to make that choice. Although Jesus loved him, He was quite prepared to accept any decision the young man made. This should be our stance in all our relationships. True love is not afraid of the consequences of standing for principle. Rather, it says humbly, yet resolutely: I'm sorry, but my principles are not for sale. Are you tempted to lower your standards to land a job, to secure a business deal or to get a life companion? Are you compromising your standards in your home, among your friends, or even in the church? I challenge you today to lovingly and respectfully stand for principle and leave the consequences with God. While unity, acceptance, and peace are desirable goals in all human relationships, they should not be bought with the compromise of principle.

True Love is Limitless

There is a second dimension to this concept of true love: it is limitless. It is willing to go all the way in the interest of the one loved. Such love holds no reservations and is willing to make any sacrifices, unlike the young man in the following story.

Two young lovers were strolling casually down a country lane one afternoon. They were both in high spirits and were exchanging words of tender affection to each other. The young man said to the young lady, "Sweetheart, I am prepared to face death for you."

She responded, "Oh honey! That's so sweet to hear." Just as the words were out of her mouth, a ferocious dog scaled a fence and began to move angrily towards them, barking in menacing tones. This young man, sensing the imminent danger, took to his feet with amazing speed, leaving his beloved alone in her plight. The young lady began to scream and tried to keep the dog at bay by grabbing her shoes off her feet and waving them at the dog. Fortunately for her, the owner of the dog ran out and called the dog back and so no harm came to her.

A block down the road, the two lovers met up again with the young lady still panting for breath. In consternation, she asked him, "Honey, I thought you said that you will face death for me?"

"Yes, sweetheart," was his response, "but that dog wasn't dead!"

God's love is limitless and He, indeed, faced death for us.

God loved the people of this world so much that he gave his only Son (John 3: 16).

In Christ, God gave His all for the human family. All heaven was wrapped up in that one gift.

I gave my life for thee My precious blood I shed
That thou might ransomed be And quickened from the dead
I suffered much for thee
More than thy tongue can tell
Of bitterest agony, To rescue thee from Hell
I gave, I gave my life for thee, What hast thou given for me.
("I Gave My Life for Thee.")

Jesus employed tough love to withstand denial by His own disciples and scathing abuse from the religious leaders. It took tough love to accept to be spat upon, to be beaten with many stripes, and to be unceremoniously ridiculed. It took tough love to resist the temptation to use His power to strike down His tormentors.

It is no joy to have your motives questioned, your morality in doubt, or your mission distorted. To come to your own and to have them reject you is not easy to bear. A self-centered love would have given up and returned to heaven. Such selfish love would have said, "I don't have to take this. Who do they think I am?" Selfish love says, "Why must I do this for you? Why must I do you any favors, for I am not your servant or your slave?" A selfish love looks at how much is given in relation to how much is received. It sets limits on its giving, for it only gives to get. Such love is basically self-serving for it has "I" as number one. Such people love themselves first and foremost.

Through it all, the tough, selfless, and sacrificial love of Jesus remained strong and resolute. His love never moaned or groaned, and it never said a mumbling word. The world's greatest lover was unyielding in His determination to bear the Cross, to shed His blood, and to save the human race.

Our Lord knew what He was doing. He went in with his eyes wide open. In fact, He predicted what would happen in verses 32-34 of Mark 10. His actions were not based on mere feeling or lovesick sentimentality, but on fixed principles and a commitment to go all the way for His beloved. This was a limitless love – a love without boundaries. This is a love that never leaves you nor forsakes you, a love that will not let you go. Praise God for such love today!

Tough love demands a principled response. Jesus saves *from* sin, not *in* sin. In responding to the love of God, indeed to any lover, there has to be a leaving and a cleaving, for true love demands a loyal response. Jesus challenges us to keep His commandments if we love Him, for the test of love is loyalty and obedience. If we love Him, we will strive to please Him. Indeed, if I love my spouse (which I certainly do), I will seek to please her as long principle is not being compromised.

True Love is Self-Controlled

This brings me to the final dimension to this concept of true love. True love is principled, it is limitless and equally important, it is based on self-control. In all our love relationships, we need to set the standards and leave an open door. No one should feel that they *have* to love us. No one should be trapped in a relationship in which they feel that the day they leave, disaster will strike!

No matter who it is (sweetheart, spouse, or child), and no matter how much you love that person, no matter how dependent you have unwittingly become on that person or that person has become on you, true love requires that you set your standards and open the door. Take control of yourself and the relationship for love is not blind; neither is it some emotional frenzy devoid of common sense.

I am not talking here about merely a mistake or a wrong action for which the individual accepts responsibility. Rather, I am talking about a wayward attitude. John, the beloved disciple of Jesus, wrote that if any man sins, he has an Advocate with the Father. The understanding is clear; therefore, if we have done wrong, there is mercy with the Lord. Similarly, we must be willing to bear with the wrongs of our beloved if they acknowledge, confess and forsake.

Cherished sin is a different matter. Our loved one must know that despite our deep, abiding love, we will not tolerate waywardness. We will not uphold them in their wrongs. We will not stop loving, for love alters not when it finds alteration, but we will not condone and support. Jesus continued to love that rich young ruler, but He did not lower His standards to gain the young man's love. Neither should we. Love thrives best in an atmosphere of mutual respect. When respect goes, love dies. True love is principled, limitless, and self-controlled.

Too many parents bemoan the problems they face with their children today, but they are, at times, afraid to hold up the standards. Some modern psychological theorists posit the view that children should grow up virtually unrestrained, and when they are older, they will eventually develop the required social behaviors. Further, state governments are now placing additional restrictions on parents in terms of the disciplining of their children. In such a context, the child becomes the master of the man and in many homes today, instead of parents training children, children are now "un-training" their parents.

Mothers and fathers, let me remind you that you represent God before your children. You are to reflect both His mercy and His justice. Your firm, yet kind discipline is necessary if they are to become well-adjusted citizens in this life and eternal citizens in the kingdom of God.

The State may legislate, but it cannot build character. A failure by parents to maintain their standards in raising their children has led to many homes off-loading their untrained, undisciplined youngsters on society and many of these end up as wards of the courts and the penal systems. The Word of God is clear: *Teach your children right from wrong, and when they are grown, they will still do right* (Proverbs 22:6). That training involves disciplining.

I encourage all parents to set standards in your homes. Set standards for home duties, for children need to learn that life is not just a joyous merry-go-round playing video games, or being engrossed with their media devices. Set standards because children operate best within clearly defined boundaries. Protect them from themselves, their feelings and their friends. Set standards for their conduct and expect them to be upheld.

Your child may rebel, s/he may accuse you of lack of love and understanding, or of being too restrictive and living in the nineteenth century, but I encourage you to set the standards and leave an open door. Since they are in your home and you are responsible for their support, they need to abide by your standards. In the future, they will love and respect you for this.

Let me also address the issue of that husband, wife or sweetheart who is making life a misery for you. You are not first in their affections, but you are not free to go, neither do you wish to. You just seem to be dangling like a puppet on a string. They are primarily in love with themselves or with another but remain happy to have you just there on the wings, in waiting. You are like the spare tire in the car!

What must you do if you find yourself in such a situation? First, I suggest prayer. Ask God to change you, to strengthen you and to sanctify you. Is there any wicked way in you? Ask God to forgive you and cleanse you for, although sin is solely the sinner's fault, you may be partly responsible for predisposing him/her in waywardness.

Secondly, make sure that the issue is one of principle, and not just a matter of personal habits or preferences. How many major family fights and even divorces can be traced to trivial issues? She is angry because he always leaves his shoes in the sitting room, and he is hitting the roof because she always squeezes the toothpaste from anywhere and creates messy spills! In these issues of personal habits, while you are free to state your preferences, you will need to learn to be patient and to accept human differences. Matters of principle, however, must be taken seriously.

Thirdly, I suggest that you make every effort to communicate to your beloved how you view the situation. Use "I" language rather than "you" language. Set your standards. Outline your expectations. Your love must be limitless, but it must not be unprincipled. Say what you mean and mean what you say. Pray constantly that God would give you the grace and wisdom to speak in a manner that will glorify His name. Don't bottle up your feelings. Let your partner know in as Christ-like a manner as possible where you are hurting and what, in your judgment, needs to be done to rectify the situation.

Fourthly, open the door. Let the person know that you love him/her, but you do not love the waywardness. The language and tone of Dr. Dobson's sample letter, quoted earlier, will make the point quite clearly. You desire them to remain, but their waywardness must go. We are talking about tough love. S/he must choose between you and the waywardness, and you are quite prepared to abide by whatever decision is made. You may even indicate that you will be sad to lose him/her, but God is gracious. He will heal and restore and give you grace and strength to face the future.

Finally, never give the impression that your life will fall to pieces if your loved one leaves, for your sense of wholeness and your source of support come from God, not any human being. You have been placed here on this earth to reflect God's love and character. Therefore, retain your self-control, dignity and independence, for your beloved does not carry around your oxygen! It is *in Christ* that we live, and move, and have our being. *Why are you here?* I am here to love as God loves.

CHAPTER SIX

For Adults Only

After the round of lovely speeches at a wedding reception, the young bridegroom rose to his feet and proclaimed why he got married. He claimed that he tied the knot because, while marriage has many pains, singleness has few pleasures. Many, of course, will not agree with his point of view. I have been to weddings where there were big ceremonies surrounding the regretful departure of the bride and groom from the society of single sisters and the bachelors' fraternity, respectively. Evidently, some still think that singleness is a preferred option. However, both married and single folks are subject to periods of trials and triumphs in their lives and in their relationships. In whatever state you are in, the key is to find peace and wholeness first with your God, then with yourself, and finally with those in your world. This chapter is dedicated to assisting spouses and singles achieve these objectives.

Spouses

I love weddings. I get excited about the overflow of emotions, energy and enthusiasm. The preparations, the pomp, and the pageantry impress me. I am charmed by the glitter, the glamour and the grandeur of such occasions: a blushing bride, a nervous groom, anxious loved ones, beautiful maids, handsome gents, happy couples, supportive friends and well-wishers, and hopefully, glorious weather. Another union is made, another family established and the model from the Garden of Eden continues.

Regrettably, there are some whose only comment on my enthusiasm for marriage is, "Wake up! This kind of storybook romance you are talking about doesn't exist today." They say, "For me marriage is a life sentence, hell on earth, and at best it's a peaceful coexistence. You live your life, I live mine." The following are real-life scenarios that are brought into evidence as support:

- ☐ My husband is having an affair with another woman and claims he doesn't love me anymore.
- ☐ My wife has gone to the Frigid Zone emotionally and she keeps telling me to take more cold showers whenever I approach her.
- ☐ My parents are always arguing, fighting and throwing stuff at each other. If that's marriage, I don't want it.

Yes, these are the sad realities today. It is important, however, to revisit the Biblical ideals in the light of these current realities.

Marriage is a lifelong miracle! In Genesis 2, we read of the pairing of the animals but *none of these was the right kind of partner for the man* (Genesis 2:20).

Thus, God put him to sleep and, taking a rib from his side, He made woman for man. Then God issued in *verse 24* what I regard as the ideal for a happy marriage. *That's why a man will leave his own father and mother. He marries a woman, and the two of them become like one person.*

Leave and Cleave

In the above verse in the KJV, God challenges spouses to leave and cleave. This is the first requirement for a successful marriage. Spouses need to leave all emotional ties of the past and place their partners as No. 1. in their lives. Parents can no longer be No.1. Old friends must now take second place. Former interests and hobbies must now be mutually agreed upon and integrated into the new lifestyle. You can't truly cleave until you fully leave. One husband was complaining to me in a counseling session that his wife does not regard him as a priority. She claims that the children must be first and he will understand, even when the children are young adults!

Marriage is the severing of the umbilical cords of past and extraneous emotional ties and the start-up of a new life, a new union — each for the other and both for the Lord. It must be the paramount desire of each spouse to work to promote the happiness of each other. You plan together, pray together and pursue life's interests together.

Whenever I reflect on my own marriage, I never cease to give God thanks for my wife, Martha. Her family has always been a closely-knit one and they grew up quite interdependent on one another. I was more the lone ranger, independent type. As I saw the closeness of their family, I asked myself the question: Are her sisters and mom going to co-manage in my home? I did not have to wait long to find out.

When we got married, Martha was able to cut that emotional navel string quite quickly and cleave within her new family unit. Our future was ours to decide under God. As a family, we made some major decisions, and we moved quite a lot. We moved from Trinidad to the United States for study, then to England, back to Trinidad, back to England and back to the United States. In the US, we moved from Atlanta, GA to Walla Walla, WA, then to Riverside, CA, to Trinidad as university president, and then back to GA. More recently, we have been commuting between Atlanta and the U.S. Virgin Islands in connection with my role as a professor at the University of the Virgin Islands.

In all these decisions, however, it was always what was God's will for our family. While Martha has continued to love and value her parents and siblings to the fullest and we enjoy getting together whenever we can, she certainly lived out the Biblical principle to leave and cleave. I love her for loving and valuing me to that extent. For her, it was a matter of first committing herself to God and then to her marriage.

Some spouses ask whether they lose their individuality when they get married. The answer is both no and yes. You are not to become a carbon copy of your spouse, forced to like what s/he likes and dislike what s/he dislikes. Christ died to preserve your individuality and it ought not to be surrendered to any other person–not even a spouse. The Holy Spirit speaks to you as an individual and you are called upon to give an individual response to God's claims upon your life.

On the other hand, a kingdom divided against itself will not stand and this holds true for the kingdom of the home. While you remain different persons, there needs to be interests, priorities and activities which may be pursued together. In this scenario, there will be the need for mutual understanding and compromising, for both cannot continue to do exactly what they were doing before they met each other and still maintain a marital union. For the marriage to work, both have to leave and cleave.

Love and Submit

The second requirement for a successful marriage is found in Ephesians 5:22-31. In sum, we are called to love and submit. To submit means to yield one's rights. This gives some men a sense of power and a thrill in the spine as they assume that their wives have to yield their rights to them. The cursory reading of this text plays to our masculinity, but the submission spoken of here is not servitude. She is partner, not property. Secondly, submission is not forced, but springs naturally, for wives are to submit to their husbands as they do to their Lord. Our Lord does not force anyone to submit to Him and neither should we.

Submission does not suggest the absence of dialogue since communication is a vital part of any relationship. Both parties must be able to talk with each other lovingly, truthfully, and respectfully. You must be able to share with each other your innermost feelings, your joys and sorrows; your hopes and hurts; your triumphs and tears.

Interestingly, men are also called upon to submit. In *verse 21,* we are told: *Honor Christ and put others first.* In *verse 25,* men are called upon to love their wives as Christ loved the church. This is a call to care for, to provide for, to protect, even to give one's life for, if need be. The submission is, therefore, mutual. She is to yield her rights willingly out of love for him, but he is to be willing to yield his life out of love for her. She demonstrates her love in submission, and he demonstrates his submission in love. She pleases him by all means and he displeases her by no means. He rules her from the head, and she rules him from the heart. All this, of course, is a pattern of the relationship between

Christ and His church. The church is able to sing "All to Jesus I surrender," ("All to Jesus I Surrender.") because Christ is already singing, *I gave my life for thee, My precious blood I shed.*

The reality is that this kind of mutual submission becomes unworkable when it is not reciprocated. It is easy to love when you are loved in return, but how much greater a challenge it is to love when your beloved fails to return that love. Wives, I could understand the struggles you have to be submissive to one who is not loving towards you — to one who is just not worthy of your love. Husbands, I can imagine how difficult it is to love a woman who is of a strong, independent spirit and just does not seem to care. How does the Bible speak to these situations? We are to submit, not because of the response of the other person, but out of reverence to Christ.

The love of Christ is the inexhaustible fuel for Christian love. His love knows no boundaries. His love has no limits. He gives and He gives, and He gives again. That's the model for us in our marriage relationships. I firmly believe, upon the authority of God's Word, that *the solution to most marital problems is to love some more.* So often, whenever conflicts arise, we cease to love. We go silent or we hurl verbal and, at times, physical abuse. We move to the other room. We go our separate ways. This is to the delight of the devil.

We are here to love, and that love demands that we keep the channels of communication open. It could be that my spouse is right, and I am wrong. Therefore, we learn to give in out of love for each other. However, some of us are too stubborn to admit that we are wrong. We senselessly prefer to create disharmony in our union rather than simply say, "I am sorry, I was wrong". Sometimes, the issue at stake is such a trivial one that you wonder why a conflict developed in the first place? Why break up a marriage over the color of the new carpet or whether you squeeze the toothpaste from the top or the bottom? Let us be prepared to lose some battles and win the war over a broken marriage. Love and submission melt the hardest hearts.

Another worrisome feature in our litigation-frenzied society is the prenuptial contracts that protect partners if the marriage does not work. While the experiences of many make one sympathetic to these precautions, it does seem difficult for a marriage to survive when it is seen purely in terms of a contract. Marriage is more than a legal contract with clearly circumscribed rights and responsibilities. More fundamentally, marriage is a spiritual commitment. It goes more than fifty percent. If necessary, it goes all the way. In a sense, your marital love makes you vulnerable since your love is based on a sense of oneness and trust. When trust goes, the marriage is over. You may remain together, but it's never the same.

Pray and Trust

Ephesians 5:18 provides us with the third essential requirement for marital happiness. We are encouraged to keep the atmosphere of heaven in our hearts and our homes. Be spiritual leaders. Trust your spouse, for the more you watch, the less you see. Leave him/her in the hands of Jesus. Be the best and let God do the rest. Very importantly, don't give your spouse the feeling that s/he is being caged or imprisoned. The most flourishing relationships are those where both parties have the space to be themselves and voluntarily choose the companionship of each other. If I feel caught, cornered or caged, I will seek to be free. Some spouses become so desperate and possessive that their partners have no room to breathe. Open the emotional cage door and let him/her choose. Whatever they decide, find your peace, worth and wholeness in Christ. A spouse must never feel that s/he is a captive in the marriage. Strive to promote each other's happiness.

All of this requires a certain Christian maturity. This is why marriage is not for children. Ephesians 5: 19-21 encourages us to fill our lives with psalms and hymns and spiritual songs and to be always in the spirit of thankfulness and praise. Such a positive, joyous Christian spirit could override many hurts and deficiencies in relationships and maintain the sunshine of God's love upon the marriage.

Love is patient and kind, never jealous, boastful, proud, or rude. Love isn't selfish or quick tempered. It doesn't keep a record of wrongs that others do. Love rejoices in the truth, but not in evil. Love is always supportive, loyal, hopeful, and trusting. Love never fails! 1 Corinthians 13:4- 8

This is the kind of love we are called upon to exhibit in our homes as sons and daughters of God.

SINGLES
People are single for different reasons. Some choose not to be married. Others keep this option open but have not yet found the right companion. Still others have had singleness thrust upon them, having lost their loved ones through divorce or death. Whatever the reason, God loves singles just as those who are married and so should all of us.

There is a tendency for some married folks to distance themselves from singles. Several factors are responsible. Some of these include:

- [ ] the need to protect your name or that of your spouse. In our suspicious age (and this is not always without foundation), a male entering the home of a single female or vice versa immediately causes eyebrows to raise and questions to be asked.
- [ ] the inability to understand or relate to the needs of singles.
- [ ] the view that since singles and married folks will obviously have different agendas, they must be kept separate.

These factors have all contributed to creating distance between singles and those already married. As a result, a common plight of most singles is loneliness and a sense of alienation from the church community, the body of Christ. Some are made to feel guilty for their singleness and are encouraged to pray and fast to get out of that condition. I was at one church where the first elder invited all the married members to stand and hurled various accolades upon them. He then said to the singles that he did this to make them jealous so that they, too, could hurry up and get married. I felt pain for every single in that congregation! Singles are frequently teased as to when is their wedding date; who they are dating now; or, with a suggestive grin, the question is posed, "Is everything okay?"

The church family needs to learn how to minister to the singles in its midst. Singleness is not a sin. It is not a physical or emotional malady. It is not one of the seven last plagues. Singleness is a status we have all experienced and may again experience through choice or circumstance. Singles are no different from anybody else and they should be fully incorporated as full-fledged members of the family of God. The best friends of Jesus were three singles: Mary, Martha and Lazarus. While marriage remains the Biblical ideal, singleness remains a wholesome option. We must remember that Jesus was never married, neither was the apostle Paul.

Practical Suggestions for Singles

Cast all your cares upon the Lord

Let me proceed to provide some practical suggestions for singles. First, I present the Lord to all of us. *God cares for you, so turn all your worries over to him* (1 Peter 5:7).

This is particularly comforting when you are in a situation where you feel that the church does not understand or care. Everyone, whether single or married, needs to find their sense of self-worth and wholeness in Christ and not from how they are perceived by others. While compliments, acceptance and good favor are to be cherished, they ought not to be the barometers of our spiritual and emotional wholeness. We must come to the point where we are neither elated by applause nor dejected by rebuke or censure. That is the Jesus model.

Start Living /Stop Existing

In John 10:10, Jesus reminds us: *I came so everyone would have life and have it fully.*

There are two words for life in Greek, *bios* and *zowe*. *Bios* refers to mere existence, such as breathing and blood circulation. On the other hand, *zowe* suggests the enhanced lifestyle, the more abundant life or fullness of life. For those singles who are depressed, discouraged and hurting because of their current status, I implore you to review your state and take steps to find meaning and fulfillment in life as it is for you at present. Do not worry about what tomorrow may bring: spend your energies in making today as fulfilling and satisfying as possible for yourself and for your world.

I had to share the above counsel with one of my senior female church officers. One morning as I approached my vestry to prepare for the church service, I saw her at the side in deep tears. I took her into the vestry, and she talked in tears about her frustrations at not being married. All her friends were now married, and she felt that she was being left on the singles shelf. She just couldn't stand it anymore. I really felt sorry for her, but apart from listening, encouraging and praying for her, there was little I could have done. She had to be encouraged to begin viewing life differently and to find meaning and contentment in her present state.

Similarly, I counseled a forty-year-old man who was having difficulties in cementing a lasting relationship and this was bringing him great frustration. He earnestly desired to marry, but his advances were frequently met with rebuffs.

Jesus remains the source and circumference of our happiness. As a single person, God has endowed you with beauty and brains, life and health, opportunities and time. Go forward and fulfill your desires, pursue your dreams, reach for your stars. You can be alone, but you do not have to be lonely. Get out of your pj's, switch off the phone or the TV, stop eating junk and gaining weight and get a life. In whatsoever state you find yourself; therewith be content. Visit friends, go back to school, get involved in church or a community initiative, and/or visit places of interest. Value and celebrate your independence. If a prince charming or lady beautiful is to catch you, let him/her catch you on the move. Believe me, s/he would be impressed!

Start Sharing, Stop Sulking

Some singles give the impression that they are always fighting the world. They often give the signal that, *It's me versus the world!* Just go near them and you will feel the fire of their venom. They constantly moan and groan about injustices around them and what needs to be put right. I say to such folks: lay down your armor. Develop a positive, selfless attitude. The world is not round but flattened on both ends. Everything is not perfect. Learn to ignore some perceived hurts and move on. Insults and hurts are taken, not given. Forget the negatives and get involved in helping others. You can:

<u>Share your time</u>–helping the sick, the elderly or the children

<u>Share your talents</u>–in music, in witnessing or in church office

<u>Share your resources</u>–with the needy and in support of mission projects

Don't Compromise your Principles

The counsel of 1 Timothy 5:22 is quite important. It advises us: *Don't sin because others do but stay close to God.*

You will be tempted to drop your standards, just as we all are tempted to do. Owing to a sense of loneliness, the encouragement of friends or other factors, you may be tempted to join in questionable conduct and practices that are contrary to your professed standards and convictions. Some young men and women engage in drug-taking, violence and free sex just to add thrills and excitement to their lives. Sometimes, after lives have been scarred and reputations sullied, sadder but wiser, they ask themselves the question: *"What were we doing there?"*

Even in bona fide relationships that have the potential for a positive future, you may be called upon to compromise your standards. One young man said to his young sweetheart that he would not marry her unless he first was able to test the equipment, as he couldn't afford to buy "a dog in a bag." Unfortunately, she succumbed to his line, and when he was through, he wanted neither the dog nor the bag. Sexual promiscuity outside of marriage is no basis for building sexual faithfulness within marriage.

Sometimes there may be a sense of remorse at not lowering your standards, as your friends may have done, but please do not succumb to such reasoning. After her former boyfriend went off and married another person, a young lady I counseled said to me that maybe if she had consented to sleep with him, she might have been his wife today. I had to respond that while that may have been so, the opposite was equally possible and, in any case, it was a shaky foundation on which to build a lasting relationship. How would you know if sleeping with someone would result in marriage? And what kind of marriage could that be if it is built on your pleading for a yes from him because you have given him everything? Your dignity, self-respect and the Word of God all say *wait*. In Philippians 4: 19, we are reminded that *My God shall supply all your needs*.

In conclusion, let me emphasize to both spouses and singles that we can be sufficient in Him. He is the center of our joy. Personal happiness and fulfillment are not found so much in finding the right person as it is in being the right person. *Always let him lead you, and he will clear the road for you to follow* (Proverbs 3:6).

Ultimately, God is calling individuals to salvation. As individuals, therefore, we all have our challenges of faith as we seek to live a godly life in a godless world. We have a heaven to gain, a hell to shun, a God to glorify and a worthwhile life to fulfill. Success in this undertaking for singles and for those who are married lies in knowing God for ourselves and growing daily in Him. That's what we ought to be doing here!

Alternative Lifestyles

I cannot finish this chapter without treading into the area of alternative lifestyles. This has been an area that has challenged the beliefs and behaviors of even those within the Christian community. Earlier, I referred to the experience of Pastor Ontay Johnson and his wife Gina when their son came out as Kiah, a transgender female. While the pastor continued to struggle with the reality of his child's decision, his prioritization of Christian love in the situation is commendable. *What would Jesus do?* has been my North Star as I pondered on some of these controversial issues that confront the church.

Let me assert that I believe in the Biblical model for marriage as set forth in the Genesis account. However, I also do recognize that there are many who believe otherwise. All are entitled to their convictions and the consequences arising from them. My stance, however, is to always seek to be a loving and lovable Christian; to always seek to model the Christian lifestyle. The gay or lesbian is a person; the transgender is a person; all persons who subscribe to any of the alternative lifestyles are persons and their lives do matter as well.

We Christians teach that Christ died for all. To hear that an activist Christian man will arm himself with a pistol at the church door to prevent any members of the LGBTQIA+ community from entering the church is a clear misunderstanding of the Gospel he seeks to advocate. For a Christian preacher to assert that "they must not bring their junk into the church" demonstrates an abysmal lack of Christian grace and the redemptive power of the Gospel. Sure, the alternate lifestyle deviates from our Christian beliefs as understood from the Bible, but is it possible to love the person irrespective of their beliefs and behaviors? Is it so difficult to love unconditionally? What would Jesus do?

CHAPTER SEVEN

Thank You

Every year, we look forward to the Thanksgiving holidays. This is a time set aside for us to focus on giving thanks and expressing appreciation to God and to one another. In reality, though, thanksgiving should be a way of life for the Christian all year through.

We are reminded in 1 Thessalonians 5:18: *Whatever happens, keep thanking God because of Jesus Christ. This is what God wants you to do.*

In Psalm 103:2, we are encouraged: *With all my heart I praise the Lord! I will never forget how kind he has been.*

In Luke 17, Jesus was on the border between Galilee and Samaria, where He was approached by 10 lepers. No one was to touch them, and they were to keep their distance from those not stricken. The leper had to live in isolation from society, and if they saw a healthy person approaching, they had to shout, "Unclean, unclean," to warn the person not to come closer. The leper had no home, and generally no future. It was a miserably hopeless condition. In this group of pitiable outcasts were nine Jews and one Samaritan. Normally, these two groups wouldn't even come close to each other, but now they huddled together in their common woe. The disease had obliterated all distinctions of race and class.

How often we find that when life is bright and beautiful, we are not as sensitive to some people around us as when we are ill, or in some form of distress. We then look for help and support from anywhere. The drowning man does not ask the man on the bridge throwing down the rope, "Are you black or white, gay or straight?"

The lepers knew that they were in a hopeless condition. It was rare for anyone to return to their homes after contracting leprosy. Thank God they met Jesus, the Greatest Physician. They cried unto the Lord and He heard their prayer. It is so reassuring to know that with God all things are possible. Jesus healed them of their malady and, as the custom was, sent them to the priests for their certificates of cure.

What excitement for the men as they went to the priest! Their limbs now responded with great ease, the sensations of health vibrated throughout their bodies, fresh currents of blood now jetted their way through their reactivated veins. Thank God, they were healed, cleansed, and restored. What particularly interests me, however, is not the healing of the ten lepers by Jesus, but their responses to this healing. Jesus had made it all possible! Their lives were now markedly different because of what Jesus did. They were immediately transformed from the grim prospect of a hopeless end to the joy and exhilaration of endless hope — all because of Jesus. A miracle had been wrought, new life had been achieved, the unimaginable had occurred. In response to this new lease on life, I want to dig deeper into their differing responses. I want us to reflect upon the inaction of the majority, the reaction of the Master and, finally, the action of the minority.

The Inaction of the Majority
Nine lepers left the priest filled with a joyful sense of elation, but little sense of gratitude. Their thoughts immediately turned towards home, family and the future. They counted themselves lucky to be healed but forgot the One who made it all possible. One can picture them now, busy with their thoughts on how they would make up for past time and lost opportunities.

How often we, too, forget to say, "Thank you." Our darling spouse goes to great lengths to prepare that lovely meal or build the extra cabinet and we simply take it all for granted without ever remembering to say *thanks*. Children lean on their parents for everything and when they grow older and have achieved, they show such scant regard for the sacrifices of their parents, even being ready to thoughtlessly dump them into the first senior citizen facility they can find. Colleagues may have assisted us, opening doors and supporting us in our climb up the career ladder. Do we remember to say *thanks*, or do we take it all for granted? How quickly we forget those who have blessed and benefited us along the way.

When was the last time you said, "Thank you"? It is always a sobering sight to witness funerals where people are shedding buckets of tears over the dead but failed to really appreciate the person before s/he died. Let us throw flowers when people can still catch and smell them. When last have you said *thank you* to your wife, your husband, your children, your parents, your friends, your loved ones or even to your God, who makes all things possible? The question is meant for sincere reflection. This is a vital part of what you ought to be doing here.

A final point that is worthy of note is that the nine lepers were all Jews — like Jesus. This may not have been a significant factor for them, but I find it interesting that sometimes it is your own people who take you most for granted. We endeavor to be so polite and proper to strangers, to extend all the courtesies, to even go that extra mile, yet we tend to be short and sharp with those in our inner circle. The boss gives flowers to his secretary and abuses his wife. The wife sees the good qualities in other men, but only the defective traits in her own husband. One preacher's wife said she enjoyed going to church just to see her husband laugh – with others!

The Reaction of the Master

Jesus reacted to the lack of appreciation by the nine healed lepers. He asked in Luke 17:17: *Weren't ten men healed? Where are the other nine?* This question suggests that Jesus expected all of them to say *thanks* and was disappointed that nine didn't. However, Jesus was not unduly surprised, for He knows the nature of the thoughtless, selfish human heart. Even so, Jesus was emphasizing a basic Christian expectation.

Thankfully, the inaction of the majority in expressing appreciation did not cause any paradigm shift in the attitude of Jesus. He who made man in the beginning knows what is in man, and His love is not dependent upon the response. In actuality, He does not react, for He acts the same way whether we show appreciation or not. His love is constant and consistent. I wish I could be like my Lord in this regard, because my human nature tempts me to be nice to those who are nice to me and to be short and sharp with those who take me for granted. If you are honest with yourself, I believe you will also admit to similar temptations.

Hopefully, we can reach the stage in our spiritual development and maturity where we do good, not because of the thanks we receive, but because it is good to do good. We ought to be able to do good for goodness' sake and not because of the applause or lack of it. Was it William Shakespeare in Sonnet 116 who wrote: *love is not love which alters when it alteration finds*, (Poetry Foundation, "Sonnet 116: Let Me Not to the Marriage of True… | Poetry Foundation.") I am so thankful that we serve a God who does not stop giving, even when we are not grateful for His blessings. His blessings are as unconditional as His love.

The Action of the Minority

The parable in Luke 17 indicates that only one leper returned to give thanks — and he was a Samaritan. He was from across the tracks, from despised and dispossessed people, from the poor and the powerless in society. While the Jews were considered a people of privilege, the Samaritans were an ejected and rejected people. They were victims of religious bigotry and social isolation. Nonetheless, it was a Samaritan who returned to give thanks.

Contrary to the popular view, the Samaritans had much for which they could be commended. As we discussed in an earlier chapter, it was a Samaritan who demonstrated Christian love to an injured traveler. It was a Samaritan who demonstrated witnessing zeal after Jesus opened to her the joy of salvation at the well. She raced to her city and shouted to all in John 4:29: *Come and see a man who told me everything I have ever done! Could he be the Messiah?* Now in this story in Luke 17, a Samaritan returned and, with a loud voice, glorified God for a new life in Jesus. He just couldn't keep it quiet.

How could you be quiet about a God who washed your sins away; turned your nights into days; lifted your burdens; calmed your fears; and with His own handkerchief of love dried your tears? How could you be quiet about a Jesus who brought you from small-town USA, from the cotton-picking plantations and farms of the south, from European provincial obscurity or from some desolate Caribbean or African village?

I don't know about you, but I am so thankful to God for bringing me a mighty long way. Growing up as the youngest child of a single parent in rural Trinidad, and seeing none of my older siblings attend college, I was set for a similar path. We all lived in one-room where five of us either slept crosswise on the bed or took turns on who got the bed and who hit the floor.

Nevertheless, God had other plans. I know where I came from, and I know who has blessed me all along the way. I am thankful to Him for the career He chose for me and saw me through. I am thankful to Him for family, for friends, and the many whose lives He has allowed me to touch and enrich. I am thankful to Him for health, hope, and happiness. Above all, I thank Him for the promise of a better tomorrow – eternal life when He comes again. Like the healed Samaritan leper, I just can't keep it quiet! Thank you, Lord!

Why are you here? You are here to say *thank you* to God and to all those who have blessed and benefited you along life's journey. Be generous in your expressions of appreciation and thanks. Is there someone you need to thank today? Like the Samaritan, return to say, "Thank you."

CHAPTER EIGHT

The Returning Rebel

Let me begin by asking you a very sensitive question. How do you respond to the wayward behaviors of a loved one? How do you respond to a child who no longer wishes to follow your directives, but is bent on a path of rebellion? How do you respond to a spouse who has been unfaithful? How do you respond to a trusted friend or church member who has been maligning your good name and has disappointed and even embarrassed you?

In Luke 15, we read about a young man who was bent on a wayward path. He chose to ignore his father's directives and preferred to secure his portion of his father's heritage and leave home. When you are young, you often think that you know everything that there is to know. Many times, you would listen to no one, especially adults. You reason that they have lived in a previous generation, and therefore couldn't possibly say anything that could have relevance for your life today. Your peers become your primary points of reference. This young man in the story evidently felt more for the desires of his dudes than for the directives of his dad. His fast life of fancy clothes, sports cars and fine women doubtless brought much pain and suffering to the father's heart. He loved his son and earnestly desired him to follow the path of rectitude, but he couldn't force him. I know many fathers and mothers go to bed with tears in their eyes because of their wayward children. Some spouses are living in daily emotional pain owing to the immoral behaviors of their partners. In other aspects of wayward behaviors, there are loved ones who cheat you out of positions or possessions. There are those who abuse your body or your good name. There are so-called friends who disappoint and discredit you.

Let me just interject a few words on parent/teen relationships. The stage between childhood and adulthood is one that brings trauma, especially in many Christian homes. It is a difficult time for both the teenager and his/her parents. The child is no longer a child, but not yet an adult. There are questions and confusion over their changing needs, their changing physiques, and their changing expectations. The child is preparing to throw off all parental restraints, while the Christian parent is reluctant to loosen the reins of control until the parent is quite sure that the child is mature enough to act independently. This normally leads to tensions. The young person may become moody, miserable, and depressed while the parent may become harsh, frustrated, and angry. If this period is not handled carefully, it could lead to major problems. One mother said to me that she was so exasperated over the behavior of her daughter that, as a frustrated mother, she was ready to drive her car into a huge tree in the median of the motorway and end her life. On the other hand, some young people, seeking to burst free from parental control, make some serious errors that affect them throughout their lives.

To parents who have been driven out of their peace and prosperity by the inexplicable behaviors of their teen and early 20s children, perhaps an understanding of the brain functions of young people could be helpful. The brain functions are not fully developed until a person reaches the mid-20s. The part of the brain behind the forehead, called the prefrontal cortex, is one of the last parts of the brain to mature. Do you know the main functions of the prefrontal cortex? This area is responsible for skills like planning, prioritizing, exercising self-control, and making good decisions. Wow! Many youngsters get involved in all kinds of crazy stuff simply because their fully developed prefrontal lobes have not yet arrived. Amazon hasn't yet delivered this package! This understanding of the brain function helps us to better understand, but not justify, the failures and foibles of our youth.

Every person has been created with the ability to choose right from wrong. We may encourage and persuade, but we cannot force anyone to follow our wishes. As our children grow older, our approach to managing their behaviors must lean towards more reasoning and discussion of options rather than the issuance of unquestioning fiats. Obviously, we must take the appropriate actions to protect ourselves from further hurt or loss, but the will is the sacred domain of its owner. We cannot force anyone into compliance. Sometimes, in our righteous indignation we may wish to shake or even bully others into submission, but that usually proves to be counterproductive. What we must continue to do is to pray for our loved one and let love lead.

If we accept that the most, we can do for a wayward loved one is to lovingly encourage him/her to change and to pray for that person, how do we respond when that same person decides to change and now wants to return into our good graces and fellowship? This was the situation with the prodigal son. He ended up in the pigpen of life, and there he came to recognize that even the servants in his father's house fared better than he was doing at that time. The Bible records those telling words in Luke 15:17: *"Finally, he came to his senses."*

What a joy and relief it is to have loved ones come to their senses, for them to recognize that they have hurt and disappointed others, they have wasted their time, energies and resources, and have abused privileges and opportunities is truly a major relief to their loved ones. Sometimes, the Lord has to place us in difficult circumstances so that we may be able to pause and have this inner conversation. That voice of the Spirit that had been trying to reach us and had been unsuccessful owing to our crowded agendas now finds the time to interact with the inner being and eureka! Victory is gained and the person comes to him/herself. This young man was now sorry for what he had done and wanted to go back home. The question becomes: how do you respond to the wayward who desires to leave their pigpen of error behind and return into your fellowship? There are typically three responses to the above question.

Leave Them There

Some people argue that since the wayward person made his/her choice, s/he must now remain with it. The adage, "As you make your bed, so you lie in it," is cited. As a parent and/or loved one, you have experienced hurt, shame and loss. You have suffered ridicule and deprivation as a consequence of the wayward person's actions, and so you feel justified in closing the door on their return. It almost seems easier to psychologically remove that person from your life, and thus believe that s/he no longer exists.

In an issue of the *Adventist Review* several years ago, Pastor Ron Halvorsen tells the story of a young Christian girl, a pastor's daughter, who ended up living in some rough New York City apartment. She grew up in church and was actively involved. However, as she got older, she began to mix with the wrong crowd, who enticed her away from home. She crisscrossed the United States, moving from her home in California and ending up in New York. She got pregnant and eventually had a young child.

While in New York for an engagement, Halvorsen learned about her and decided to pay her a visit. When he approached her apartment door, he could hear the music booming from the inside. He pounded on the door until she opened. When she learned that he was a minister, she was uninterested, but he persisted in wanting to talk with her. Finally, she allowed him in. As they talked, he learned of her wayward living but found that she was now coming to her senses. However, she could not return home because her father had disowned her. She therefore felt that the bridges back to her home and her father's heart were all burnt.

Refusing to accept defeat, Ron Halvorsen went home and called her father in California. "I just visited with your daughter," he began.

The voice on the other end replied, "I do not have a daughter!"

Halvorsen was astonished at the response and, his anger rising, said to the pastor, "You are a liar, for you do have a daughter and a lovely grandchild."

The girl's father broke down and began to talk about his ideals for his daughter and his disappointment at her life course. He finally agreed to allow his daughter to return home. Halvorsen arranged for the daughter and her child to return to California and move back to her parents' home. She was pleased to return home and back into the family fellowship. She also returned to her church and subsequently met and married a Christian young man. Thank God she was not left in that dingy New York apartment.

No matter how painful the wayward acts may have been, we cannot, in all Christian conscience, ignore the efforts of one who decides to make a move in the right direction. The prophet Isaiah, reminding us of God's care for the struggling, wrote in *Isaiah 42:3*:

> "He won't break off a bent reed or put out a dying flame,
> but he will make sure that justice is done."

While God is just, He is also loving. If you take one step towards the Savior, you will find His arms open wide. There is rejoicing in heaven over one soul that repents. We cannot leave them there in their pigpen.

Forgive, but Don't Forget

Some others relate to the returning rebel by adopting the attitude that we can allow him/her back into our homes, but we must always remind them of what they have done. One husband indicated that early in his marriage he was unfaithful to his wife. It was an affair for which he was deeply sorry and sought her forgiveness and understanding. She agreed to forgive him and to continue with the marriage. However, he claimed that for years afterwards, she still refused to have anything to do with him romantically, for she remained hurt over what he had done. Counseling did not help the situation. The husband felt like a prisoner in his own home. He wanted to remain faithful to his wife and his God but, although they still lived in the home together, they no longer lived together in the home.

Folks who have strayed away from church and later returned have oftentimes been told that they must sit quietly and prove that they are truly repentant first before they are fully accepted into the church fellowship. The reformed alcoholic or drug addict, the converted ex-con, the unwed mother, all have had to prove their worthiness before they can be fully accepted. Sometimes they are never fully accepted! The returning wanderer often gets the message: you may come in, but we still don't trust you.

In *Acts* 9, how long did Ananias take to fully accept the reformed Saul as a brother in Christ and to anoint him for church leadership as the apostle Paul? Wasn't it our Lord who has promised to cast our sins into the depths of the sea and remember them no more? If God chose to remember our sins, as we sometimes seek to remember those of others, how would we stand? Let us follow our Lord in lovingly and unconditionally forgiving our returning rebel.

Forgive and Forget

I admire the approach adopted by the father of the prodigal son. He was doubtless a Jewish leader — a pastor or church leader by today's reckoning. He never associated with the pig; he never came close to one. He was obviously embarrassed by the ungodly escapades of his son and, as the news about his son's misdeeds filtered back into the assembly, he must have wished many times for the earth to open and swallow him from the shame. However, when this same son was ready to make a move towards home, the father was ready to accept him. The Word of God proclaims in *John 6:37*: *"Everything and everyone that the Father has given me will come to me, and I won't turn any of them away."*

Verse 20 of *Luke 15* indicates that the father noticed his son approaching and ran to meet him. The father had compassion on his son and fell on his neck and kissed him repeatedly. The Greek word used suggests that the kiss was not merely a polite greeting of tolerance. No! The father kissed his son repeatedly in a spirit of joy and thanksgiving. I would like to think of the kisses under three categories.

The Kiss of Love and Acceptance

The young man, ashamed for the wrongs he had committed and the shame he had brought on his household, began a speech indicating his willingness to function as a hired servant, but he never got to finish it. The father's joy interrupted his son's words. He placed his son at the center of a new day of rejoicing. By his words and actions, the father clearly indicated that he was reaccepting his son with all the rights and privileges of his former estate firmly intact. The Bible says in *Zephaniah 3: 17* that our Lord *"celebrates and sings because of you, and he will refresh your life with His love."* Isn't that truly amazing? God will celebrate and sing because of you!

The gospel of Jesus is redemptive. It is built on hope and acceptance. It is advertised by a broad smile, an outstretched arm, and a warm kiss. It is based on a genuine love for the returning person and a desire to show them the forgiving love of God. I remember a troubled 16-year-old young lady whom I visited at her home one day. When I got there, she came to the door with the sexiest hot pants I had ever seen. It was covering the barest essentials. She also wore a tube top that barely covered her upper body. Her fingernails and toenails were all brightly painted, and she had a huge chain around her neck. Before I could begin, she said to me, "Pastor, I want you to drop my name from your church roll." I looked at her, smiled, and invited her to have a seat. She sat down with a very erect, defensive stance and a scowl on her face, awaiting my response.

I simply said to her, "Your dress does not bother me. Jesus loves you and so do I." She was astonished at my response!

The young lady and I talked at length about her struggles and her fears as she grew into adulthood. I had several further visits with both her and her mother. She was dealing with a lot of guilt, rejection and anger. Over time, she came to experience the amazing grace of God and I am happy to say that she never left the congregation. Indeed, she became a singing evangelist and became quite active in the church. We must communicate love and acceptance in our speech and actions. They shall know we are Christians by our love.

Already bruised and battered by the world, by circumstances, by sin and by the devil, those who make faltering steps back to us, back to the Christian community, back to the home, and back to God need all the encouragement they can get. They certainly do not need any further whipping or sordid reminders of how evil they were. Let us assist them to give glory to God and to cement their faith in Him. Our loving Lord has promised in *1 John 1:9* that *"if we confess our sins to God, he can always be trusted to forgive us and take our sins away."* He wants the sinner to make a clean break with the past and start anew with Him. Our role is to demonstrate God's love by offering the kiss of acceptance to the returning rebel.

The Kiss of Forgiveness and Restoration

Acceptance must include genuine forgiveness and complete restoration. The young delinquent pondered hard and long before returning to his father. He prepared a speech to recite in Dad's presence, but the father's exultation swallowed up his son's words of remorse. Micah asserts that our loving Lord will *"trample our sins and throw them in the sea,"* (Micah 7: 19).

Desmond (not his real name) was tried for murder. His charges were reduced to manslaughter and, after a few years in prison, he was released on good behavior. While in prison, Desmond was visited by a Christian Bible study group and learned of the forgiving love of God. He became a Christian in prison and was overjoyed to begin his new life as a Christian after his release. Desmond was particularly fascinated with the forgiveness of God.

He would read his Bible, and anytime he found any mention of God's forgiveness he would shout, "Hallelujah!" He carried his Bible with him everywhere, and wherever he had a spare moment he would read from it. It didn't matter where he was, once he saw a relevant text, he would shout at the top of his voice, "Hallelujah!" One day he was reading his Bible while waiting in the dentist's office and suddenly jumped up and shouted, "Hallelujah!" This caused some consternation among the staff and other patients, especially when he repeated it a few minutes later.

The receptionist, seeking to be diplomatic, inquired as to why he would shout that particular word. He explained that he had experienced the forgiveness of God in a special way and so he just had to shout whenever he read about forgiveness in the Bible. The receptionist then politely suggested that instead of the Bible, he read from one of the magazines on the table. He reluctantly agreed and picked up a copy of *National Geographic*. Desmond was quiet for a while and the receptionist felt that she had taken care of her exuberant patient.

Then it happened! The sound of, "Hallelujah!" again reverberated through the office. The receptionist looked up in astonishment and inquired from Desmond why he shouted, since he was not reading from the Bible. He explained that he was reading an article in the magazine which pointed out that the deepest part of the ocean was over six miles deep. He then remembered the Bible text that said that God would cast our sins into the depths of the sea. He was so overjoyed to know that his sins were now so far from him, he shouted, "Hallelujah!"

Once the sinner forsakes, the Lord is willing to forgive. The prodigal son's past was canceled, his present was adjusted, and his future was now guaranteed as a full-fledged member of his father's household. We must be prepared to maintain an open door for returning sinners and even be willing to meet them along the way. It takes a lot of courage to make those steps homewards. We should not make it more difficult by our coldness, cynicism or indifference.

The Kiss of Intimate Fellowship

While the son was obviously overjoyed to be accepted back into the family and to be genuinely forgiven for his past mistakes, I believe that the hosting of a party in his honor must have really dumbfounded him. To hold a celebration for someone demonstrates real appreciation and oneness. In hosting the celebration, the father was also setting the tone for the young man's full acceptance by all. He who was hurt the most had forgiven the most. There was, therefore, now no reason why the young man could not be fully accepted by everyone else. We first receive the right hand of fellowship from God before the right hand of fellowship is extended from his people.

Before I close, let me make a brief comment on the older brother in this story of the prodigal son. This older brother also had some issues. Indeed, I like to think of him as the prodigal in the house. He had missed the real priorities in life. His was a religion of *dos* and *don'ts*! He was cold, legalistic, and unloving. He had little regard for his younger brother, who he claimed wasted his father's money on prostitutes.

This elder brother was so engrossed in notching up brownie points for his good works that he could not appreciate the joy of forgiving grace. He needed to recognize that his father loved him for who he was and not for the works he performed. Yes! True love manifests itself in positive works, but our Heavenly Father does not stop loving when we stop working. Our best good is not good enough and thus, for the older as well as for the younger brother, their love and acceptance by the father came as a free gift of grace.

In a sense, both brothers misrepresented the father's love. The younger said that the father's love was too restrictive and controlling and so he wanted to be free. After an ill-disciplined life that brought so much misery and pain, he came to recognize his error. On the other hand, the older brother believed that his father's love for him was dependent upon how good he was. Perched on his stilts of self-righteousness, he couldn't see how the father could find any time or sympathy — not to mention forgiveness — for a wayward son. Both sons had to understand, as so many genuine Christians need to today, that in God mercy and justice kiss each other. Both qualities are uniquely blended in the character of God. True love sets the standards for justice but thank God, it also gives an open invitation to the returning sinner.

Amazing grace how sweet the sound
That saved a wretch like me
I once was lost but now I am found Was blind but now I see.

Is there someone you need to forgive today? Is there a loved one who is hurting because of your unwillingness to forgive and accept him/her back into your fellowship? Why not open the door and let that person back into a restored relationship? That's what we are to be doing here!

SECTION THREE
TO LEARN

"Stop doing wrong and learn to live right"
–Isaiah 1:16, 17

In this third section of *Why are you here?* I focus on the Christian's obligation to keep on learning, growing, excelling, and empowering oneself. In developing the concepts, I look first at the spirit of winners or overcomers. The concepts are then elaborated upon from the experiences of a heathen king and David, the God-fearing shepherd boy. In the final chapter of the section, I use the parable of Jesus about the woman who lost her precious coin to pull the strands together and make some relevant applications for Christians today.

CHAPTER NINE

THE SPIRIT OF OVERCOMERS

There was a young man who seemed to possess a strong religious desire, but found it difficult to maintain his commitment to his Lord. He would attend every evangelistic meeting in the town, and whenever a call was made to commit one's life to the Lord, he would rush down the aisle with hands upraised yelling, "Fill me, Lord! Fill me, Lord!" He then would appear to be on a spiritual high for a few days, but soon returned to his old, unconverted ways of illicit sex, illegal drugs and other regrettable practices. After he had gone down the aisle several times uttering his prayer, and yet went back to his old ways, one cynical member of the audience who knew the young man well decided that she had to respond to his prayer. One evening, as soon as he prayed, "Fill me, Lord!" she yelled from the back of the hall, "Don't do it, Lord. He leaks!"

That young man had a strong desire to gain spiritual victories, to be an overcomer, but his deeds did not match his desires. I have also had problems in matching my deeds to my desires.

When I was a junior high school student, Gary Sobers of Barbados was the top cricketer, Pele of Brazil the top soccer player, Muhammad Ali the top boxer, John F. Kennedy the President of the United States and Roger Gibbons from Trinidad my top local cyclist. At one time or another, I had visions of being like every one of them. I saw myself scoring boundaries like Sobers, goals like Pele, punches like Ali, political points like Kennedy and cycling victories like Gibbons.

These visions of grandeur were not matched by my deeds, however. In cricket, I invariably batted at No.11, if at all, and my unorthodox left-arm spin posed no terrors to opposing batsmen. My cycling was average, and I avoided anything that smelled remotely of a ring fight. As for being a soccer player, well, let me share an experience.

During my third year in high school, I was picked (if that's the word to use, for there was no one else to choose) by my class team to play a soccer game against another class. The captain placed me in the left back position, which seemed to be quite an appropriate description for me as the events later revealed. I did not touch the ball for the entire game. It did come close at times, but somehow feet and ball never connected, not even by accident! Fortunately, my side did win the game.

The next morning, we were basking in the glow of our victory when a good friend of mine who had not witnessed the match asked the captain the embarrassing question, "How did Valley play?" I wish he hadn't asked such a silly question. After all, couldn't he see we won the game? I waited nervously for the captain's response. He must have spent time in England, because he answered with typical British diplomacy, "He didn't play badly!" The real truth was that I didn't play at all!

It is not wrong to dream the impossible dream. It is not wrong to seek that unreachable star; it is not wrong to desire the highest mountain, whether literally or symbolically, but you have got to then rise and make your dream a reality and match your desires with your deeds.

So often we hear people making all kinds of excuses for their failure to achieve their goals. They blame their circumstances, their parents and teachers, their poverty, or the color of their skin. They blame everything and everyone else when their real problem may well be that they leak! They are long on desire, but short on deeds. They can always tell you what they are going to do or wish to do, but they are not so eloquent on what they have actually done. The question is: how do you overcome when you keep on leaking?

First, we must recognize that man is helpless but for the power of God. Even so, Divine power is available to enable man to achieve. Therefore, I speak not so much of the greatness of man, but of the power of God working through man. Listen to the Word of God:

"You satisfy the desires of all your worshipers," (Psalm 145:19).

"Good people will get what they want most," (Proverbs 10:24).

"Everything you ask for in prayer will be yours,
if you only have faith,"
(Mark 11:24).

"Ask, and you will receive. Search and you will find. Knock and the door will be opened for you. Everyone who asks will receive. Everyone who searches will find. And the door will be opened for everyone that knocks," (Matthew 7: 7-8).

Therefore, dream big dreams, but let them be those that God can bless. Yes, have desires, but let them be holy desires. Seek to be and to do the best with your life, but let the motive be to glorify the name of God. Strive to be a blessing to His people; to uplift humanity; to relieve suffering; and to point people toward the way of peace and eternal happiness in the Lord.

One of the ringing truths of Scripture is that God wants us to succeed. He affirms in *3 John 2*: *"I pray all goes well for you."*

Whether you are a student, a homemaker, an unskilled worker or a professional, God wants you to achieve through him. Without Him, you will surely fail. *Deuteronomy 28: 13* lays the basis for success: *"Obey the laws and teachings that I'm giving you today, and the Lord your God will make Israel a leader among the nations, and not a follower. Israel will be wealthy and powerful, not poor and weak."*

When we are following the Lord's will for our lives, we may with confidence pray, "Fill me, Lord!"

Now that we have looked at God's part in the success equation, let us look at our part. In this section, I wish to look at three convictions held by all those who are successful. These summarize the spirit of all winners or overcomers:

I am somebody
I can do something worthwhile with my life
I will stick to it till I get there.

In summary form, these convictions read as follows: Through the enabling grace of God, I am I can; and I will.

I am Somebody

God made you unique and special. You are of value to Him — He does not make trash. You have a right to be here. Do not let anyone make you feel apologetic for your existence. Society may want to place limits on your abilities and your opportunities, but do not surrender to any limits that your God has not set. You were made in the image of God with abilities, gifts and potential. You are somebody and you are special because of this! All lives matter to God!

At times, we may be tempted to distrust and dislike ourselves. We associate ourselves with failure, deprivation and misery, and we often become victims of self-fulfilling prophecy. Some of us have been brought up in cultures of underachievement and failure and so we are led to think very little of ourselves and of our worth as human beings.

Do not wallow in self-pity. Let us learn to accept one another and ourselves, for God has accepted us. Irrespective of our history or our heritage, be assured that you are special to God. Equally, let us be quick to affirm one another, build one another, and encourage one another. The same heat that melts butter hardens clay. We can choose to be victors from, rather than victims of, our past.

I Can do Something Worthwhile with My Life

The second conviction of the overcomer is that I can do something worthwhile with my life. Paul emphasized this element of "I Can" in *Philippians 4: 13: "Christ gives me the strength to face anything."*

The average human being uses up less than 5% of the brain matter he possesses. That's like spending less than $5 out of $100. Therefore, there exists an abundance of unused brain potential in all of us. So set lofty goals and rise to the challenges in the name and power of Almighty God.

Wendy Stoker was a 19-year-old student at the University of Florida. One year, she came second in the state diving championships, carried a full study load, and found time for bowling and water-skiing. The most remarkable thing about Wendy, however, was her typing. She typed forty-five words a minute — with her toes! Wendy was born without arms, but she believed that she could still do something worthwhile with her life.

It has been said that genius is 1% inspiration and 99% perspiration. This may well be true, as it certainly takes a lot of discipline to achieve any success. Whether it is learning a game, playing an instrument, getting high marks in a subject or building a successful career, it is only through trials that you triumph in the end. Getting through life is like riding a bicycle — you won't get far unless you keep pedaling.

Malcolm Gladwell's third non-fiction book, *Outliers: The Story of Success,* was published in 2008. Throughout the book, Gladwell references the "10,000-Hour Rule." Gladwell viewed the rule as a key to achieving world-class expertise in any skill. To a large extent, practicing the correct way for a total of around 10,000 hours was a common factor for most successful people.

Some people are unwilling to exercise the discipline necessary for success. They are easily frustrated when they do not succeed on their first attempt. Thomas Edison, however, had 10,000 failures before he got it right. Since then, his light bulb has brightened the world. John Bunyan was languishing in Bedford prison in England, but that did not stop him from writing that classic in English religious literature, *Pilgrim's Progress.* Continue to believe that you can be a success, even when failures and obstacles appear in your path.

If you think you are beaten, you are.
If you think you dare not, you don't.
If you like to win, but you think you can't,
It is almost certain you won't.
If you think you're outclassed, you are.
You've got to think high to rise.
You've got to be sure of yourself before You can ever win a prize.
Life's battles don't always go
To the stronger woman or man,
But sooner or later the one who wins,
Is the one WHO THINKS "I CAN"!
("A Quote by Walter D. Wintle.")

I Will Stick to It Until I Get There

The final conviction of the overcomer is: I will stick to it until I get there. Determination, perseverance, and stick-to-itiveness are vital qualities in your march to success. Do you know what the real genius of the postage stamp is? Well, it sticks to one thing until it gets there!

The founder of the Ford Motor Company, Henry Ford, and his wife were celebrating their fiftieth wedding anniversary when a reporter asked him, "What is the formula for staying married for fifty years?"

Henry Ford replied, "My formula for marriage is the same as for making cars. Stick to one model." Marcus Garvey was the son of a stone-breaker on the Jamaican railroads. Dr. Martin Luther King was born into a humble preacher's home in Atlanta, Georgia. John F. Kennedy withstood years of bitter prejudice to become the first Roman Catholic President of the United States. Nelson Mandela spent 27 years as a prisoner on a deserted island but came back to become the president of South Africa and the engineer of the world's most fascinating experiment in racial integration. Barack Obama, the son of a Nigerian immigrant, rose from relative obscurity to become the first Black president of the United States of America. They all held on to their dreams, believing that if they stuck to it, they would ultimately get there. Winners never quit and quitters never win!

Sallie Terrell, one of my church officers in Covington, Georgia, was one of those who did not believe in quitting. She suddenly fell ill from diabetic neuropathy. She underwent two major heart operations and was left paralyzed from the waist down. The doctor told Sallie that she would never walk again, but she never accepted that prognosis. I first met her in her wheelchair one year after the accident. Her first words to me were, "Pastor, this situation is only temporary."

Although the medical prognosis remained, Sallie was determined to walk again. I saw her several times and she maintained a beautiful smile and a serene composure. She was focused, determined and assured — the qualities of overcomers. A few months after I first met Sallie, she gave up the wheelchair and began using a walker. Within nine months after I first met her, my telephone rang one day, and Sallie was on the other end of the line. "Pastor," she blurted out. "Guess what?" I instantly felt I knew what she had to say. "I made my first few steps today! I am walking again!" She was so overjoyed and so was I. We praised God together. In a few more weeks, the walker was gone, and Sallie was fully on her feet, walking! Winners don't quit and quitters don't win.

Let me issue one caution. While it is true that the path to success and excellence will be a difficult one at times, learn to enjoy every step of the way. Do not be so anxious for the victories of tomorrow that you cannot be at peace with yourself today. Also, you may see those who are climbing faster than you and others who are climbing slower than you. Do not worry about either group. Just do your best and leave the rest with God. In your pursuit of your goal, take time to smell the roses along the path.

What are your dreams? If you have none, ask the Lord to place a vision in your life — a vision of who you can be and what you can become by His grace and enabling power. Do not be discouraged by your present performance, but rather be challenged by your future possibilities! Pray our opening prayer, "Fill me, Lord!" and He will!

Our Lord himself knew that the only path to success lay in total dependence upon His Heavenly Father. He who changed water into wine, raised the dead, and walked out of the garden tomb reminds all of us in *John 5: 30*: *"I cannot do anything on my own."* Ultimate power comes from God. Every success comes from him. Every achievement is stamped with his blessing. *Acts 17:28* reminds us: *"He gives us the power to live, to move, and to be who we are."* He wants us to succeed.

On our part, we can keep from leaking, from failures, and from frustrations by inculcating the spirit of the overcomer. Why are you here? I am here to be a success, to be an overcomer, for I am somebody, I can do something worthwhile with my life, and I will stick to it until I get there. I am, I can, and by God's grace, I will.

CHAPTER TEN

A CALL TO EXCELLENCE

It was several years ago. In my youthful exuberance, I sat glued to my portable black-and-white television set when it happened. Muhammad Ali knocked out his opponent and copped the world heavyweight boxing title for the third time. In utter ecstasy and triumphant jubilation, he screamed to the excited reporters and cameraman, "I am the greatest! I am the greatest! I am the greatest!" Millions of Ali fans around the world, including me, joined in the victorious chant, "Ali's the greatest!"

Such an open display of self-aggrandizement is obviously unacceptable for the Christian; but is it possible for the Christian to seek and achieve excellence and still glorify his Maker, and not himself? Let us explore this issue by looking first at the Biblical record of a heathen king of Babylon by the name of Nebuchadnezzar.

The ancient city of Babylon (where the modern city of Bhagdad now stands), was long regarded as the capital of the Mesopotamian region. Although a mere ten miles in circumference, it had become known as an international center of commerce, trade and industry. Her inhabitants referred to her as "the origin and center of all lands."

In his book, *The Bible as History*, Dr. Werner Keller says of Babylon, "*its ancient power and glory had no equal in the ancient world,*" (p. 289). Isaiah referred to the city as "*glorious and powerful, the pride of the nation,*" (Isaiah 13: 19). This was Babylon, the great ancient city and her builder, her master and her king was Nebuchadnezzar.

From all accounts, Nebuchadnezzar was very much like Saddam Hussein or some other modern-day despot. This ancient king was a raging conqueror, a proud autocrat, a compulsive builder, and a blazing frontiersman. He moved with style, drama, and authority. He came across as a compelling commander with a selfish, unrelenting hunger for honor and greatness. In *Daniel 4:30* we can see him beating his chest and exclaiming,

"*Just look at this wonderful capital city that I have built by my own power and for my own glory!*"

Some may wonder why such an avowed megalomaniac should be brought before us. "What does he have to teach us?" He's certainly not a positive role model! We will quickly turn the page from this proud ancient despot, but I plead for a moment of tolerance even for this strong-willed leader. Maybe we should not write him off completely, as I see in him a character trait that is worth reflecting upon and may be instructive for our Christian journey.

In Nebuchadnezzar, we see someone who never settled for less than the best. He had to be the first, the best, and the biggest ever. It is clear that he had the wrong motivation for he seemed to be on a continuous ego trip. He was zealous only in promoting himself for the admiration of men, and to receive worldly praise and attention. You can probably name some world leaders like that today.

On the other hand, a committed Christian should be motivated by a deep love for God and a desire to glorify His name. Yes, Nebuchadnezzar's motivation, like that of others so inclined, is not acceptable for the Christian, and should be rejected outright. However, what about Nebuchadnezzar's striving to be the best in all that he attempted to do? Could there be something positive about this, given the right motivation? I believe so. Note the following passage.

"But you must always act like your Father in heaven,"
(Matthew 5:48).

Isn't our Father in heaven the best in everything he does? Add to this the following statements from my favorite author, Ellen White:

"Be content with nothing less than perfection,"
(<u>Messages</u> to <u>Young People</u>, p. 73).

"The Lord requires perfection from his redeemed family. He expects from us the perfection which Christ reached in his humanity," (<u>Child Guidance</u>, p. 477).

"Glorious is the hope before the believer as he advances by faith toward the height of Christian perfection!"
(<u>Acts</u> of the <u>Apostles</u>, p. 53).

Thus, a striving for excellence should be the motivation of every Christian, not to promote self but to glorify God. There should be that determination to be the best and do the best.

This perfection refers to excellence at every stage of life and in every area of activity.

Again, I emphasize that this is not for the sake of earthly plaudits and trinkets, not for the enhancement of one's position or prestige nor to be seen by men and the world, but to glorify the name of our Maker and our Redeemer. To do less is to be negligent in our stewardship obligation to our Lord. In the book, <u>Testimonies to the Church</u>, Vol. 3, p. 160, E. G. White wrote:

> *"It is a duty we owe to our Creator to cultivate and improve upon the talents he has committed to our trust."*

James 4: 17 affirms that *"if you don't do what you know is right, you have sinned."*

Another way of expressing this concept is: "To him that could be extraordinary but contents to be ordinary, to him it is sin." Yes, a dedicated Christian will want to be as perfect a human instrument as is possible through the grace of God and for the glory of His name.

A gang of masons was engaged in laying bricks near roof height in a huge cathedral. Just before quitting time, one of the workers told the foreman that he had just noticed that a row of bricks was out of line. "What should I do?" queried the worker, as he thought about having to redo the whole row.

The foreman took a brief look and said to the worker, "Nobody will see this all the way up here. Just leave it alone!" Sometime later, this construction team was on another project when again a fault was detected in the workmanship. This time the foreman's response was, "We are not building a cathedral-just leave it alone!" How many times have we offered up work that could have been done much better if we had only disciplined ourselves to be satisfied only with the best? Everything we do ought to be autographed with excellence.

We are under a divine mandate to aspire to excellence to settle for nothing less than the best, not for self but for service.

"God paid a great price for you. So, use your body to honor God," exhorts the apostle Paul (*1 Corinthians. 6:20*).

God's love simply leaves us with no choice. Inspiration provokes perspiration. Our pursuit of excellence is an inevitable consequence of our commitment to the Lord.

We glorify God when we stretch our minds and bodies to the fullest. That same Creator who unravels to man the mysteries of space and the marvels of modern AI technology challenges His stewards to rise higher than the highest human thought can reach. Pastors, parents, seniors, and young people, we all must let a sense of professionalism characterize our efforts and let personal growth and achievement be evident in our lives. Even when failures visit us, as surely, they will, let the world see that we can grow from them rather than haplessly mourn our misfortunes. If we had failed to rise again after our first failed efforts at walking, we would still be creeping around today.

It needs to be reemphasized that these achievements are not possible as solo efforts. Success calls for the union of divine power with human effort. Both God and man have separate and distinctive roles to perform in achieving success. We know that divine power is always assured. The critical issue, therefore, revolves around human effort.

The "plus ultra" constantly urges us forward. Forever improving are the Christian's watchwords. Even in eternity, Ellen G. White says there will always be *"new heights to surmount, new wonders to admire, new truths to comprehend, fresh objects to call forth the powers of mind and soul and body."* (*Great Controversy*, pp. 677). Thus, growth and excellence will eternally challenge the Christian.

Returning to Nebuchadnezzar, we find that his failure lay not in his God-ordained desire for excellence, but in his failure to acknowledge God and to pursue excellence to reflect God's character. Nebuchadnezzar's focus was on me, myself and I. As a steward, he had denied the reality of his Owner and had usurped the glory due only to God. This was a tragedy, and so it will be for any of us who fail to recognize in our achievements the God who gives us *"the power to live, to move, and to be who we are,"* (Acts 17:28).

There was a second failure in Nebuchadnezzar's experience. He had set himself up as the source of excellence when he was merely a reflector. The deafening "hurrahs" of men stimulated his selfish ambitions. Regrettably, he failed to point his followers to the God of his talents. His failures, therefore, lay both in his denial of God and in his coveting all the glory for his achievements.

Nebuchadnezzar's kingdom was taken from him, and he was afflicted by the disease of lycanthropy. This continued for seven years until he recognized that: *"God Most High is in control of all earthly kingdoms and that he is the one who chooses their rulers,"* (Daniel 4:32).

This is an important lesson for all of us today. No matter how bright the light, it will go out if separated from its source of power. I pray that we will be freed from the failures that ruined this ancient king. Every success involves a productive partnership between God and man. Let us always do our best for our Master, knowing that He is always doing His best for us.

THE FELLOW THAT'S DOING HIS BEST

You may talk of your battle-scarred heroes,
Of martyrs and all of the rest,
But there's another I think just as worthy
The fellow that's doing his best.

He doesn't wear gold braid and tinsel,
Nor ride on the wave's highest crest;
But he's always where duty demands him
This fellow that's doing his best.

No trumpet blare tells of his coming,
For fame he is never in quest;
But he's surely a hero of heroes
This fellow who's doing his best.

—*Author Unknown.*

CHAPTER ELEVEN

Your Winning Combination

"Why do so many young, Black people today look and act like losers?" This was the question posed to me by an English reporter one day as we sat in my principal's office in North London.

My non-verbal response to her question was immediate. I stiffened in my chair. I felt the blood pumping faster through my system. I peered intently at this woman sitting before me and wondered, *who does she think she is? Is she a racist? Is she one of those who wish all Black people no good?*

As I continued to survey this young lady's countenance, however, I sensed a depth of innocent concern. I began to think more objectively about her question. Yes, in England as well as the United States where I now live, Blacks are underrepresented in most professions. We are grossly overrepresented in the prison system, and we have a high drop-out rate in the K-12 school system. Thus, while I do not agree that the "loser" spirit is restricted to any one ethnic group, I had to reluctantly concede that, despite her motives, her question was worth considering.

These concerns may be hard to swallow since they paint a somewhat dismal picture and may even be seen by some as hasty generalizations. We may also argue that there are a series of psycho-sociological factors that contribute to this picture of Blacks as losers. "We are victims of unfortunate circumstances," some exclaim, using it as a quick answer for the situation. There is no doubt that generally, Blacks in England and, more specifically, African Americans, have scored higher on all the negative indicators of mental, emotional, and economic well-being. The research work of David Williams from Harvard University (and my college classmate) has borne that out quite convincingly. I want to suggest, however, that while these external factors are real and deep-seated, success or failure in life depends a lot on our own self-concept. In other words, my beliefs and attitudes in response to my own life circumstances have more to do with whether I achieve or not. My heritage of birth, ethnicity, or family status does not have to be an insurmountable obstacle. That's the message in Maya Angelou's fascinating poem, *Still I Rise*. It is also the redemptive news of the gospel of Jesus Christ.

A Chinese tattoo vendor was plying his trade at a busy shopping center one day when this curious onlooker approached. The observer had watched several people coming up to have a sign imprinted on their chests. The sign read: "Born to Lose." The observer finally went up to the vendor and asked why people would want such a negative sign on their chest. The tattoo vendor smiled and said that they quite loved it. He then said, "You see, they have tattoo in head before tattoo in chest." The external sign is a barometer of their internal state.

The Bible presents several instances of this "loser" spirit. One is from the story of David and Goliath as recounted in *1 Samuel 17*. Goliath posed a serious challenge to the people of Israel. In *verse 10*, Goliath issued a clarion call, *"Give me a man, that we may fight together!"* The Bible records that all Israel were *"so frightened of Goliath that they couldn't do a thing,"* (1 Samuel

17:11). In other words, they were scared to death. They felt like losers and ran for cover. Goliath was too big a problem, so they preferred to chill in the tent.

Here were a people who faced a problem of immense proportions. What could they do? Running away never has and never will solve any problem–whether it be spiritual, emotional, financial, or physical. We must learn to stand up and face our problems and challenges, whatever they are. So, this hulk of a human problem bellowed out at the Israelite army from across the valley. *"Give me a man that we may fight together!"* Will God's people conquer or be conquered by this human problem? Will they be winners or losers? Will Goliath make them or break them individually, or as a nation?

I rejoice that God never places us in a position where it is impossible for us to succeed. *1 Corinthians 10:13* reassures me that: *"You are tempted in the same way that everyone else is tempted. But God can be trusted not to let you be tempted too much, and he will show you how to escape from your temptations."*

The word *tempted* here comes from the Greek word *peirasmos*, which could also be translated as *problem*. The text is saying that whatever problem we find ourselves in, He has only allowed us to be there because He knows that we are able to bear it victoriously through His grace.

In Israel's case however, there was no man — no, not even King Saul — who dared to accept Goliath's challenge. That is, no man except David. David perhaps added weight to the adage that there are old soldiers and brave soldiers, but old soldiers are never brave and brave soldiers are never old. The question is, what made this mere stripling of a youth decide to go out and fight victoriously against Goliath despite his military inexperience, the protestations of his brothers, and the fears of King Saul's senior advisors?

I believe that the answer lies in David's philosophy of life. His life was underpinned by three fundamental beliefs that serve as the source of all true success. I call these beliefs life's winning combination. These beliefs relate to his view of God, his view of himself, and his view of his impending destiny. Let me elaborate on these three beliefs.

Belief in God

First, David believed in God and in His Almighty power (*vs. 26, 37, 45, 47*). Like David, I firmly believe that God is the Author of history and destiny. He is definitely the Author of my life. Nothing happens apart from His ultimate will. He is interested in the minute details of my life and wills me to succeed. God wants me to be a winner! I say to all God-fearing people: God wants us to succeed. His Word declares:

"Dear friend, and I pray all goes well for you. I hope you are as strong in body, as I know you are in spirit," (3 John 2)

"We know that God is always at work for the good of everyone who loves him," (Romans 8:28).

"If God is on our side, can anyone be against us?" (Romans 8:31).

I remember when I started high school at Presentation College in San Fernando, Trinidad. I was an uncertain-looking eleven-year-old in grade 7. To me, the grade 12 boys looked like giants in the school. On the playing field, I sought to keep out of their way. It seemed to be the only way to ensure survival.,

I struck up a friendship with a classmate who had a big, "bad" brother in the 12th grade. I do not know whether it was because of this or despite it, but my classmate was never afraid of those big guys. He would challenge them fearlessly, even though his full height hardly reached their chests. The rhetorical question, "Do you know who his brother is?" just seemed to keep him out of trouble. Sometimes, I envied him and wished I also had a big, brave brother.

Rejoice, we *do* have such a Big Brother. His name is Jesus. Lonely youth, frustrated mother, discouraged father, depressed member, anxious leader, I say to you, "Take courage!" Our Brother is not in the 12th grade, or indeed in any earthly grade, but He has promised His people: *"I will be with you always, even unto the end of the world,"* (Matthew 28: 20).

"When you cross deep rivers, I will be with you, and you won't drown. When you walk through fire, you won't be burned or scorched by the flames. I am the Lord, your God, the Holy One of Israel, the God who saves you," (Isaiah 43:2-3).

"You treat us with kindness and with honor, never denying any good thing to those who live right," (Psalm 84: 11).

An indomitable belief in God and in His Almighty power is the first key belief in your winning combination. It was this faith that was the source of David's strength as He faced his Goliath. Such faith could be yours today as you face the many Goliaths in your life. Listen to David on his powerful and winning belief system: *"Everybody here will see that the Lord doesn't need swords or spears to save his people. The Lord always wins his battles, and he will help us defeat you,"* (1 Samuel 17:47).

Belief in Yourself and Your God-given Abilities

The second key belief in your winning combination is to believe in yourself and in your God-given abilities. David said to Saul in *verse 32: "This Philistine shouldn't turn us into cowards. I'll go out and fight him myself."*

I imagine that Saul did not quite know what to make of this youngster. He seemed so self-confident, so well assured, with such undiluted faith in God's power and in his God-given ability. Many thoughts could have run through Saul's mind. *Why not give David a thorough scolding and send him back to his sheep? No, give him a lecture on the complexities of military warfare and he will then understand why no one is out there fighting Goliath. No, no, his faith seems just too strong to accept this. Maybe, just maybe, this lad could be right. Anyway, what have I got to lose? At least it will show that I am doing something about the situation.*

This message of believing in yourself and in your God-given abilities needs to be echoed and re-echoed, especially in the ears of those within our African American communities. Our society may want to limit us and make us believe that we are underachievers and incapable of rigorous mental activity; that we are only good for sports and entertainment. We are sometimes obstructed in our entry to the professions because of a preconception that we would not be able to cope or we are stepping out of our league. I say to you, however, believe in yourself. Have the confidence that you could aspire and achieve through the grace of God. At the risk of lecturing, let me share with you three *don'ts* that are a burden on my heart.

Don't give in to self-doubt. Believe that God works through you. Believe it on the inside and show it on the outside, since the outward appearance is an index of the inner mental attitude. How you look communicates to others whether you believe in yourself as a winner or as a loser. As the saying goes, you are not what you think you are, but what you think, you are. Martin Luther King, Jr. said in one of his popular speeches: *"Don't allow anybody to make you feel that you're a nobody. Always feel that you count. Always feel that you have worth and always feel that your life has ultimate significance."*

Therefore, when you walk the city streets or the corridors of business or government, when you present yourself to prospective employers, I invite you to walk like a winner! Dress for success! Sit with confidence! Speak with conviction! Move with purpose and assurance! At all times, maintain your dignity! Remember, you are a child of the heavenly King!

Too many people walk around so pitifully that they are almost saying to the world, "I am just a worm. Crush me!" They have a terribly low self-concept and never believe that they could ever amount to much. This is a tragedy. These people become their own worst enemies. Doubtless, society has to bear some responsibility for destroying these minds through, oftentimes, subtle dehumanizing processes. A mind is a terrible thing to waste. I trust that through God's grace, we would be assured of our identity and worth as human beings.

Don't give in to discouragement. The discouraging words and responses that come, sometimes from those closest to us, can be very disheartening. That's why I like David. The criticisms of his own brother *(verse* 28) never moved him. In fact, he hardly even stopped to respond to the charges. He was single-minded on his one objective: to defeat Goliath in the name of the Lord. He was focused on his mission, and nothing was going to deter him.

My high school mathematics teacher told me repeatedly, "You will *never* pass mathematics." My driving instructor told me, "You will *never* pass your driving test." A friend of the family told me, "You will *never* remain a Christian for more than six months." A church administrator told me that there was a slim to zero chance that I would ever work for the church again after my successful lawsuit against the organization! They were all proven wrong through the grace of Almighty God. In all cases, the road ahead was rough and sometimes the going got really tough, but I remained determined to achieve.

> *"There are some things people cannot do,*
> *but God can do anything," (Matthew 19:26).*

Don't try to be somebody else. Saul wanted David to go in his armor, but David was not Saul. He had to fight his Goliath in his own way, not in Saul's way. Some try to remake themselves to look and even talk like some successful person that they admire. In dress, hairstyles, and in mannerisms, they try to mimic the successful, unconsciously thinking that they can be a success by hitching their wagons to these stars, but this never happens! Be yourself. Win your battles with your own stones.

Of course, it does help to have positive role models to inspire us. If we see others achieving, then we imbibe that culture of success. Wise parents are concerned about the friends their children choose. Young people look at successful sports personalities, entertainers, or national figures and seek to reproduce their excellence. Traditionally, teachers, doctors, and local and national political, civic and religious leaders have been lifted up as positive role models for our children. However, recent scandals that have dominated the national media have seriously shaken some of these traditional beliefs.

The very public disruptions of the long-held and respected constitutional norms by our national politicians, as well as those of several local political and religious leaders, have done much to damage our trust in our leaders. Our heroes lie, cheat and kill. The lives of so many of our leading entertainers are clouded by illicit sex, drugs, violence and greed. Many church leaders now are preaching purely for profit. Is it any wonder that so many of our young people have become so cynical and unwilling to genuinely put forth the efforts necessary to truly succeed? Instead of promoting genuine excellence in our society, we are teaching the primitive philosophy of survival of the scheming, the selfish, and the sycophants.

This absence of positive Christian role models today poses a serious threat to the transmission of our values and our heritage. The messages coming from the media, from the mixed-up lives of national personalities, and even from the man in the street are generally contrary to our Christian values and ethos. Thus, many lose the will to strive and settle for less than the best. Mediocrity largely becomes the order of the day. What a tragedy! Friends, let us always try to do the best we are capable of under God.

Belief that Truth Will Ultimately Triumph Over Error

Let me now share with you the third and final belief in your winning combination. David firmly believed that truth would ultimately triumph over error, and it was this conviction that aroused his righteous indignation. This was his motivation for action. He believed in a cause larger than himself. The love of truth, equity, and justice must be in the breast of every winner. All men and women of honor must rise and be counted in defense of these bedrock values. Whether on an individual or corporate scale, right must be pursued in preference to wrong. Herein lies the assurance of success for any Christian or any community today. The Scriptures declare: *"Doing right brings honor to a nation, but sin brings disgrace,"* (Proverbs 14:34).

The issue, therefore, becomes essentially a matter of sin or righteousness; hell, or heaven; a hopeless end or an endless hope. May I ask you then today, are you on the Lord's side? Do you believe in Him and in His mighty, saving power? Are you following His principles in your daily life? It is only as we make the commitment to live as God wants us to live that we can truly become all that He wants us to be, both now and eternally. Our destiny is being shaped by the decisions we make from day to day. That's why we must frequently reflect on our theme question: *Why are you here?*

Listen to the words of David in the first Psalm. This is his testimony as he doubtlessly reflected on the miraculous leading of God in his life and his assurance of a secure destiny through the grace of God.

> *God blesses those people who refuse evil advice and won't follow sinners or join in sneering at God. Instead, they find happiness in the teaching of the Lord, and they think about it day and night. They are like trees growing beside a stream, threes that produce fruit in season and always have leaves. Those people succeed in everything they do,* (Psalm 1: 1-3).

Therefore, I say to you, fear neither man nor circumstance. Resolve that you will not give in to life's pressures but will be a winner under God. No matter what the battles, be assured: *"In everything we have won more than a victory because of Christ who loves us,"* (Romans 8:37).

The cross of Calvary is a constant reminder that our victory is guaranteed. Once our life is in Christ, then we may claim His victory as ours. Be assured! The Lord has made a way for you.

> *I know the Lord will make a way for me*
> *I know the Lord will make a way for me*
> *If I live a holy life, shun the wrong and do the right,*
> *I know the Lord will make a way for me*
> ("I Know The Lord Will Make A Way For Me Chords-
> Twila Paris.")

Go forth therefore and be a winner! With or without the plaudits of men, you are a winner when you live as a trusting, obedient child of God. This is why you are here!

CHAPTER TWELVE

THE LOST TREASURE

By English standards, her home was nothing more than a one-room bedsit. In America, we would euphemistically call it an efficiency apartment. This was the humble home of a poor Syrian widow. The building was of ancient architecture; there were no windows and only one entrance. It was always dark and dingy. Over time, as her possessions accumulated and the room was rarely swept, the place got covered over with dirt and rubbish.

All this woman's earthly possessions were in this tiny room. Among her memorable treasures, however, was her wedding gift of ten pieces of silver stored in an earthen clay pot. As was the custom of the time, she had received this gift from her mother at her wedding and was to pass it on to a daughter in the family at her wedding to preserve the family heritage.

In the book of *Luke 15:8-10,* Jesus summarized this woman's story. I imagine that from time to time she would count the ten coins, just to make sure they all were there. She valued this treasure in the earthen vessel. Today, we also have a treasure in an earthen vessel. The book of *2 Corinthians 4:* 7 makes this point clear: *"We are like clay jars in which this treasure is stored. The real power comes from God and not from us."*

What's our treasure? Isn't it salvation through the shed blood of our loving Lord? Isn't it the joy of the new life in Christ which makes us sing, "Blessed assurance, Jesus is mine"? Isn't our treasure also the freedom to pursue our faith, our careers and our lives by God's grace?

As this woman in our story would check for her treasure from time to time, usually all was fine, but this particular day things were different. She counted only nine pieces of silver — one coin was missing! She re-checked, but sure enough, one coin was lost. This filled her with great misery. Have you ever lost something of value? How did you feel about it? This woman's loss filled her with utter misery. Let me share with you some areas where I believe treasures may have been lost by Christians today.

Lost Personal Relationship with the Lord

This Syrian woman knew she had lost something. This was no time for keeping up appearances and maintaining a tough chin when all was not well. If you lost it, admit it. That's the first step to recovery. I ask you: Is your Christian experience still the same as when you first met the Lord, or have you lost something? Is His Word still precious to you, or have you lost something? Is faithfulness and godly living still important to you, or have you lost something? Do you still believe in and uphold Christian standards, or have you lost something? If you are honest with yourself, you will know when you have lost something. If there is a lack of direction and purpose in your life, a casual attitude towards your personal spirituality and walk with God, or no passion for living and sharing your faith, you just may have lost something! This woman in Luke was filled with misery because although the earthen vessel had remained, the treasure was gone. She had lost something!

There are some Christians who are good at keeping up appearances. They maintain the forms and trappings of religion. They lead classes, choirs and committees. They perform all the religious functions — even on a full-time, professional basis – but while the earthen vessel remains, the treasure is gone. The earthen vessel of religious forms, duties and ceremonies remains but the reason for its existence — to house the treasure of God in the life and actuating the spirit — is lost. When He's absent, the rest descends to mere forms, ceremonies, and rituals. It is like having a lamp without light, form without function, and function without any holy unction. In short, external religious rites and rituals are meaningless without an internal relationship with Christ. Our power comes from God, and, without that treasure, our outward religious activities are of little significance.

That coin in the woman's apartment, though lying among dust and rubbish, was still a piece of silver. It remained valuable. If you have turned away from God for any reason, I want to appeal to you today. I do not know how you view yourself or His followers today. You may be still hurting from some unfortunate experiences. Others may have already cast you into the dust and rubbish heap of life, but I want to assure you that you are still a piece of silver in God's eyes. The Christian church may have failed you, but God has not failed you. You are still precious silver to Him. So precious are you that God sent His Only Son to die on an old, rugged Cross and He would have done it for you alone.

The good news is that this woman did something about her loss. Her misery gave birth to her mission. Jesus tells us in *Luke*

15:8 that she searched the house carefully for it. I like that! She was passionate about regaining what she had lost. Somebody needs to pick up that refrain:

> *Take* me *back, Dear Lord*
> *To the place where I first received you*
> *Take* me *back to the place where I first believed you*
> ("Andraé Crouch–Take Me Back Lyrics | Lyrics.Com.").

Take me back to my first commitment, take me back to my passion for the Lord, take me back to my love of the pure and tasteful in music, literature, and entertainment. Take me back to loving and caring for those who need my help and support. Take me back to living from fixed ethical, moral and Christian standards and not from political or financial expediency. Take me back to speaking truthfully and honestly and letting the chips fall where they may. We have lost some bedrock values as a nation, and we are worse off for this loss.

Lost People

If you were to take a census at any church assembly, you would find a significant disparity between the book membership and the actual church attendance. This reality came early for me. I was given my first ministerial assignment as associate pastor at the Stanmore Avenue Church in Port of Spain, Trinidad. At our first session together, my well-respected senior pastor, Fitzgerald Harris, passed me the membership list of over 1,600 names. He said to me, "Clinton, we have 1,600 on the books but only 600 in church. I want you to go and find the other 1,000!" I can tell you that this assignment kept me fully occupied during my short stay at Stanmore Avenue.

That assignment, and similar ones over the years, have given me the opportunity to talk with many who have left their Christian fellowship. These were husbands, wives, children, parents, relatives and friends who left because they did not feel loved, cared for or supported within the church community. Apart from those who have left, there are so many more who live and work with us but have never made a public confession of their faith in Christ. We feel free to talk to them about any subject under the sun except the treasure that is dearest to our hearts. They remain outside of the fellowship – still spiritually lost because our treasure remains our best-kept secret. We must share with others the rich treasure that we have in Jesus Christ.

Lost Priorities

A third and more fundamental issue of loss may center on our priorities as a Christian community. Where is the spirit of the pioneers today? Where is the burning sense of mission? Where is the flaming desire to know Christ and to make Him known, thereby helping to transform lives and homes and societies today, as well as prepare people for their coming Lord?

I have to ask myself some searching questions. At age sixteen, a friend and I went door-to-door, witnessing with fervor for our Lord. Times have changed and technology has leaped forward since those days, but there is a danger that we may become so caught up in the technological gadgets of our time that we find no opportunity for one-on-one encounters with one another and with our God. John Naisbitt warned about this trend in his book, *Megatrends (Warner Books, 1984, p.36)*: *"We must learn to balance the material wonders of technology with the spiritual demands of our human nature."*

We may argue that it is necessary to use the best technology to carry forward the Lord's work, and I agree; but let's get our priorities straight. The technology is the earthen vessel; it is not the treasure! I have watched the development of satellite and even Zoom technology in evangelism. The Net 98 series of the Seventh-day Adventist Church heralded a new dawn for virtual evangelism. The COVID-19 pandemic also forced many churches to upscale their technology resources to be able to share their worship services online to wider audiences. These have been great developments in the advance of God's kingdom. The Atlanta Berean Seventh-day Adventist Church now has its worship service streamed into homes in over 40 countries around the world. It is fascinating that wherever you are in the world, the same message can reach you. I believe this is undoubtedly the way forward. Still, this high-tech approach to evangelism must be seen as a more extensive means of, and not a replacement for, that personal touch of one redeemed sinner telling another sinner where to find hope. Computer and satellite technology are to be tools of, not substitutes for, the presence and power of the Spirit of God.

The absence of the Spirit is becoming noticeable in our congregations today. There is a need for a return to straight forward, Spirit-filled preaching in Christian pulpits. Preachers need to be calling sin by its right name. In the name of political correctness and fear of offending social sensibilities, too many spiritual leaders no longer speak with prophetic assurance. Many now subscribe to the view that whatever a person does must be right for him/her and no one else is to judge. If they believe it's right, then the popular thinking now says that it is right for them. The result of such thinking is that there is no wrong, for there is no absolute standard. Once we take away the ultimate standard of right and wrong based on traditional Biblical standards, we are left with anything goes! We are riddled now with fake news, alternative facts, and personal conjectures. AI technology is now used by bad actors to spread misinformation, and disinformation creating havoc and influencing opinion in dangerous ways. I fear for our young people today who are growing up in a world where standards are swiftly shifting and where the people who stand up for truth and right are often castigated and even branded as extremists. As individuals, and as a nation, we have lost our moral and spiritual compass, and this is so regrettable. Our misery must give birth to our mission to recover that which was lost.

Lost Personhood

The final loss I wish to share is of particular significance to those of the Diaspora. Five hundred years ago, we had the treasure called freedom. The Afrocentric and the Eurocentric worlds lived separate but equal lives. They experienced similar patterns of growth and development. They were nations of co-equals, but greed and deception transformed this reality into one of dominance and enslavement. The treasure of freedom was lost.

We were herded across the Middle Passage like cattle, and many lost their lives on this journey. Those who survived this ordeal were sent to plantations across America and the West Indies. We were subjected to gross indignities. We toiled hard and long and millions of our African brothers and sisters ended their days in abject servitude on the plantations. It is simply outrageous today for political leaders to be talking and seeking to educate on the benefits of slavery! Slavery was an evil that has blighted our land. It was the loss of personhood – a sacred treasure — for free people of color from the African Diaspora.

Thank God, there were some whose misery gave birth to their mission. They looked beyond the plantation fence and saw freedom beyond. They saw the prospect of regaining what they and their forefathers had lost — human dignity and personhood.

In their mind's eyes, these slaves never accepted the script assigned to them — scripts that stated that they were less than other people. While circumstantially they were slaves, in their minds they remained free. They eyed the boundary fence and determined that someday, sometime, they would make a run for it. Many did! This runaway spirit has been a feature of our Black experience. Harriet Tubman may be regarded as the icon of the runaway spirit, securing her own freedom and that of 300 others as they headed towards the northern states of America through her famous Underground Railroad.

In our society, the evils of slavery still abound and the plantation fence of old has been replaced in modern America by the corporate glass ceiling and political shenanigans. Political, economic and social slavery remain a living experience for many African Americans today. The situation is no better in the United Kingdom or across Europe, wherever ethnic minorities have a significant presence. Even so, I praise God that the runaway spirit is still alive! We are breaking through the glass ceilings and other artificial barriers set up by those who fear our power and passionate dream for freedom and equality.

May I encourage somebody to move out of your plantation of subservience and make a run for it! Do not let the sin of slavery today squeeze you into its mold. Break loose and follow your dreams. Let your misery give birth to your mission. As a born-again child of God, that's what you ought to be doing here.

There is something even greater than the sin of slavery. It is the slavery of sin! The slavery of sin robs you not only of your personhood, but also of peace of mind. It brings restlessness, not because of harsh masters without, but because of a lack of mastery within. Unlike the sin of slavery, the slavery of sin is voluntary; it is self-imposed. It is the most absolute, voluntary and self-destroying form of slavery, as it is eternally destroying. The most pitiable kind of slave is a slave to his/her own passions, weaknesses, and failures.

Again, the runaway spirit is possible! *1 Corinthians 10: 13* reminds us that whatever the problem, God has provided a way of escape; the runaway route. We can turn to Jesus, our precious Savior, in a moment and find life and have it more abundantly. The same God who redirected Elijah from his cave of hopelessness can transform your life with a glorious and hopeful future.

The woman in our story never wallowed in her misery. She was not indifferent to her immeasurable loss. Her misery gave birth to a passionate mission, and she did not cease until she found what she lost. Then the Bible records that she called her friends together to rejoice with her over finding her lost coin. Whatever coin you have lost, this story reminds us that lost coins can be found. If we seek diligently, we can find our loss and the restoration of this treasure brings great rejoicing. I do not know how long it took the woman to find the lost coin, but I can assure you that a lost personal relationship with God can be restored in an instant. The Word of God says in *John 6:37:* *"Everything and everyone that the Father has given me will come to me, and I won't turn any of them away."*

Lost friends will need to be worked with over time and they will respond differently, but if we keep a positive and supportive attitude, we may well regain many lost friendships. Individually and as a church community, there is also the need to re-focus our priorities on that which is of eternal value — our lost treasures!

So often we fight, backbite, bicker and squabble over trivial things! Let us keep our eyes on our mission: to know Christ and to make Him known. Finally, as people of Afrocentric heritage, we must lift our vistas and become what God desires us to be. We cannot change our history, but neither must we be prisoners of our history. We can determine that we will not perpetuate, nor be accepting of the relics of slavery that still exist, and indeed, seems to be on the rise. We can adjust our present and transform our future individually and as a people. Why are we here? We are here to strive for the highest ideals, having found freedom and liberation in the gospel of Christ. Again, I quote from my favorite author: *"Higher than the highest human thought can reach is God's ideal for His children,"* (Ellen White, Education, pp. 18).

And from Jesus Himself: *"If the Son gives you freedom, you are free!"* (John 8:36).

SECTION FOUR
TO LOOK

"So, Christ died only once to take away the sins of many people. But when he comes again, it will not be to take away sin. He will come to save everyone who is waiting for him," (Hebrews 9:28).

This final section of our four-part symphony takes us from the present into the future and the blessed hope for all Christians — the coming of Christ. Above all else we are doing here, we ought to look forward to this most climactic event in our world's history. I first review the biblical description of the Christian church in the last days, as recorded in *Revelation chapter 3*, and the pitfalls Christians need to guard against as they look toward that great day. The need for us to be filled with the Spirit of God as we look forward to this awesome event–the coming of the Bridegroom — is then highlighted. Chapter 15 reassures us that, despite the troubles we see and personally experience, trouble won't last. The final chapter focuses on the mission of the church as we move from the present to the glorious future realities. Our mission is active for it calls for self-preparation and the preparation of others for the glorious day of our Lord's return.

CHAPTER THIRTEEN

The Modern Laodicean Church

The ancient city of Laodicea could well be called the City of Compromise. There were no extremes, no strongly held features in the city. It was ever pliable and accommodating — full of the spirit of compromise. Situated about fifty miles from Philadelphia and about six miles from Colossae, it stood at the junction of two important roads. It was a city of wealth, with large markets, a large banking exchange, and large manufacturing interests. Laodicea was also known for its lukewarm baths and mineral springs that attracted visitors from all over Europe and Asia. An important school of medicine had also developed in the temple of Karu, and connected with this school was the manufacture of an eye medicine called collyrium.

The city itself was well ordered and self-sufficient. Black garments were worn almost exclusively by the people of Laodicea as evidence of their wealth. Partly because of their wealth, the citizens were generally found to be proud, arrogant, and self-satisfied.

The Condition of the Laodicean Church Today

Christ's message to the church of Laodicea is a message to His last-day church — the church in existence just before His return. The message of Laodicea is to a Christianized generation, cultured and educated, but skeptical, complacent and compromising. The church receives no commendation, for it has imbibed the spirit of the world around it, and its people are in spiritual jeopardy. The lukewarm baths of Laodicea were a turgid symbol of many professing Christians just prior to the return of our Lord. Note that our Lord does not charge them with hypocrisy, for a hypocrite is an imposter or a pretender — one who knows better but fails to do it.

On the contrary, the Lord says of this church that they do not know. They possess all the outward evidence of cultural attainment, yet they are actually wretched, miserable, poor, blind, and naked. They are wealthy as measured by the world's standards — possessing beautiful church buildings, wonderful institutions, and centers of learning — yet lacking the very essentials of Christian experience. When materialism eats its way into our hearts, it destroys our passion for anything spiritual. Too many people in our 21st century generation are comfortable and self-satisfied, yet we know not our real condition. We are inoculated with just enough Christianity to make us immune to the genuine thing. Could anything be more tragic? Yet, this condition prevails at the very time when our Lord is about to return.

One of the refreshing pluses for me when I became the pastor of the Atlanta New Hope Seventh-day Adventist Church is the interest the young people had in studying the Scriptures. The church had the distinction of being one of the leaders in all divisions of the National Bible Bowl Championships for North America. Bible study is no longer popular, even among Christians, and so young people who are thus engaged need to be encouraged. *"Understanding your word brings light to the minds of ordinary people,"* (Psalm 119:130). The study of God's Word makes a positive difference in people's lives.

What the meaning of the term *hot* means in the Laodicean passage is not difficult to conceive. The mind at once calls up a state of intense zeal, when all the affections, raised to the highest pitch, are drawn out for God and for His cause, and are manifested in active, sacrificial service for God and our fellowmen. To be lukewarm is to lack this zeal, to be in a state in which heart and earnestness are wanting, in which there is no self-denial that costs anything, no cross-bearing that is felt, no witnessing for Christ, and no valiant efforts in pursuit of Christ and His mission to humanity. It is living the life so prevalent among our Millennial, Gen Z and Alpha generations – the pursuit of selfish interests with minimal efforts extended towards any outside of their immediate circle. Worst of all, it implies complete *satisfaction* with that condition.

"Lukewarmness" is the cancer that is eating away at the Christian community today. Luke-warmness in the pew fosters inertia where nothing can trouble one to action. Sermons are for the other folks. Religious activities are for those who have time. Tithing and giving offerings are for those whose bills have already been paid. Honoring the Lord's Sabbath of the ten commandments begins whenever I get home on Fridays, or not at all. What is even more disconcerting is the luke-warmness that is evident among many Christian leaders still occupying pulpits across America. In many cases, they continue the routine of Christian services, but their fire has gone out. Their congregations sit and listen to men and women who claim to be bringing messages from God, but these preachers clearly have not spoken with Him in a long time!

I always chuckle when I remember the cartoon showing a man being dragged out of bed by his wife one morning so that he could attend church. "I don't want to go to church this morning," he protested.

"But you must go, honey," his wife replied.

"Give me one good reason why I should go to church today," he retorted.

"Because you are the preacher!" she painfully reminded him.

The church steeped in lukewarmness is filled with forms and ceremonies at the expense of living faith. It emphasizes policies instead of people, on money rather than mission. Such congregations put the emphasis on loyalty and longevity rather than holy zeal and commitment. Indeed, the lukewarm church frowns on any who seem to be too enthusiastic, too passionate, too eager to further the gospel. Like the city, the Laodicean church seeks to avoid any extremes. Thus, visionary plans and actions are stifled in bureaucracy and red tape and their adherents ostracized for troubling the waters. In the spirit of the Chinese proverb, the nail that sticks out is hammered in. As *hot* denotes joyous fervor, a lively exercise of all the affections and a heart buoyant with the presence and love of God, so *cold* would seem to mean a spiritual condition lacking in these qualities, yet one in which the individual *feels* a lack or a great destitution.

While coldness is preferred to lukewarmness, the Lord never desires us to seek that state. There is a far better one which we are counseled to attain, and that is to be zealous, to be fervent, and to have our hearts all aglow in the service of the King. When you are cold, there is no indifference, nor is there contentment. Instead, there is a sense of unfitness and discomfort, a groping and seeking after something better.

There is hope for a person in this condition. When a man feels that he lacks and wants, he will earnestly strive to obtain. The most discouraging feature of the lukewarm, modern Laodicean church members is that they are conscious of no lack and feel that they have need of nothing. There was more hope for the real conversion of the *cold* publicans and harlots than there was for the self-satisfied, lukewarm Pharisees who felt no need.

Laodiceans are content with correctness of religion without its accompanying power. They have structure without the Spirit, contentment without commitment, Christianity without Christ. They are long on the theory of religion, but short on practical godliness. Yet they see themselves rich and increased with goods and in need of nothing. Typical Laodicean Christians are content with the status quo and are unwilling to even entertain the idea of change. They are so proud of the history and heritage of the church that they constantly seek to relive that history at the expense of a brighter future. It is almost impossible to convince them of their great need. This is the failure of the Laodicean church. Their whole being should cry out for the Spirit, the zeal, the fervency, the life, the power of a living Christianity, but they do not!

Counsel to the Modern Church of Laodicea

What are we to do? First, we must cease trusting in ourselves and recognize our spiritual poverty. Thank God, we may purchase the riches of heaven. We may be blind, but we are not incurably blind. We may ask God to restore our spiritual eyesight. We may need to be clothed, and He is there waiting to cover us with His own robe of righteousness.

It is interesting that the cure offered to the Laodicean church directly responded to the three major godless emphases within that ancient community. The fashionable black garments worn by the Laodiceans were, to them, evidence of their superiority and self-satisfaction. However, the Lord points out that they were actually evidence of their spiritual poverty and nakedness. Therefore, we are counseled to take off the black robes of our own self-righteousness, and symbolically put on the white robes of Christ's righteousness instead. This is an acceptance of Christ as Lord of my life and my willingness to live my life in harmony with the Christian principles and values enshrined in the Scriptures.

Secondly, the black robes were also symbolic of their wealth that came from their large commercial markets and strong banking interests. The church of Laodicea today is counseled to seek rather for the "gold tried in the fire," a living, dynamic faith in God. The third counsel to purchase eye salve is also significant. It was a direct response to the so-called learning for which the city was noted. Spiritual eye salve refers to the spiritual discernment that comes from the abiding presence of the Holy Spirit in one's life.

Today, our black robes may be represented by our homes, our careers, our institutions, our prosperity or a host of other gods that we unconsciously deify and worship with our funds, time and best energies. We look to science and technology for our eye-salve; for our modern breakthroughs, and some of these are really fascinating. However, we must remember that the God of heaven and earth is the Author of science and technology. All knowledge comes from Him. It is also important to point out that, unlike the messages to some of the other churches in Revelation, no fault is found with the Laodiceans concerning the doctrines they hold. Their beliefs are correct, and their doctrines are sound. The issue is not one of doctrine, but of lifestyle — lack of spiritual commitment.

The overcomer in these last days therefore is one who, although she may have been blessed with earthly goods, does not trust in them, but rather has surrendered her all to Christ and lives by faith, reflecting God's love in her life. Filled with the Spirit of God, she is at peace with herself and at peace with the world as she waits and earnestly works for the coming of the Lord. She is a member of the church triumphant.

The Call to Modern Laodicea

So great is His love for us that the Heavenly Vendor goes from house to house plying His wares. *"Buy your gold from me,"* He pleads in *Revelation 3: 18*. He condescends to go knocking on the doors of our hearts to affect the needed reform. Notwithstanding our offensive attitude, our unlovely character, our selfish interests, such is His love that He humbles Himself to make us blessed. *"Listen! I am standing and knocking at your door," (Revelation 3:20).*

He goes round from door to door in Laodicea. Not only does He knock, but He calls out, *"you hear my voice and opens the door, I will come in and we will eat together," (Revelations 3: 20).*

It is not the person inside that is taking the initiative, but the Lord who is outside standing there, pressing against the door, pleading for entrance. It makes no difference who it is or his/her condition. The invitation is for any man. I rejoice that anybody could be a part of the Lord's kingdom, for His invitation is for everybody.

The Consequences for Laodicea

There is a two-fold promise for the overcomer in these last days. First, the Lord promises to come in and have supper with him. This suggests intimate communion and fellowship. What a joy it is to be in fellowship with the Savior, to bask in the sunshine of His presence and thereby be free from the darkness of doubts, disappointments and fears.

Hymn writer Jessie H. Brown expresses our feelings so beautifully:

> *Anywhere with Jesus I can safely go,*
> *Anywhere He leads me in this world below.*
> *Anywhere without Him dearest joys would fade;*
> *Anywhere with Jesus I am not afraid.*
> *Anywhere with Jesus, I am not alone,*
> *Other friends may fail me, He is still my own.*
> *Though His hand may lead me over dreary ways, yet Anywhere*
> *with Jesus is a house of praise* ("Anywhere with Jesus.").

Secondly, the overcomer has the privilege of sitting on the throne with Christ. Indeed, we are a royal people, as Paul reminds us. Justified by the blood of the Lamb, we now have the privilege not only of membership in the eternal kingdom, but also functioning as princes and princesses of the kingdom of God. What a glorious future! Just to be there would be good enough for me, but glory hallelujah, I've got a mansion, a robe and a throne waiting for me in glory. The Bible tells me in *Revelation 20:4* that we shall live and reign with Christ a thousand years.

The Bible is full of examples of those who persevered and were triumphant. A hungry den of lions did not keep Daniel from his daily prayers. A blazing fiery furnace did not cause

Shadrach, Meshach and Abednego to bow before a heathen idol. The virtue and virginity of Joseph was severely tested, yet his faith in God and his stand for principle stood triumphant in the end. Think also of Hannah, Abraham, Mary Magdalene, and John on the isle of Patmos. As part of the church triumphant, the able defenders of the faith and liberators of Satan's unwilling captives will keep steadily before them the blessed hope, the glorious appearing of our great God and Savior Jesus Christ.

We must be aware that the Laodicean message of these times will shake up the church in these last days. Those who wish things to continue as they were would be disturbed by the calls for reform and the passion of those who desire to remain loyal to their God. The church may appear as if it is about to fall apart, but thank God, it does not fall. Those who have been overcoming by the blood of the Lamb and the word of their testimony will stand faithful and true, without spot or wrinkle, arrayed in the righteousness of Christ. They will be steadfastly fulfilling their purpose for being here as children of God.

Laodicea means a justified people. God wants us to be justified by His grace so that we are victors and not victims; we grow and not grovel; we soar and not sink; we overcome and are not overwhelmed. This is the vision of the church triumphant. Guided, empowered and protected by God, the Laodicean or end-time overcomers will be enveloped with Christ in His glory at His Second Coming. Clothed in His righteousness, these believers will be transported to heaven where there will be no more sorrow, death or pain. God Himself shall wipe away every tear from their eyes. Glory to God in the highest! *Why are you here? I am here to live for Him, to reflect His character, and to look forward to His glorious return in the clouds of glory!*

CHAPTER FOURTEEN

Fill Me, Holy Spirit!

It was a beautiful evening scene. The sun had set behind Mt. Olives and the heavens were curtained with the shades of evening. Christ and His disciples sat on the mountaintop and looked down the mountainside. From their vantage point, they saw in the distance a brightly-lit home prepared for some festivities.

The light streamed from the window as an expectant company waited for the marriage procession to commence. In many parts of the East at that time, wedding feasts were held in the evenings. In *Matthew 25,* we learn that in that waiting company were ten young women, robed in white. They all carried lighted lamps and small oil containers. Jesus, looking upon this scene, immediately used it to help His disciples understand the nature of the kingdom of heaven. He further used the experience of these ten women to represent His church as it awaits His return.

Heaven is a Place of Joy

First, we must note that Jesus likened the kingdom of heaven to a wedding feast. It is instructive that He chose a wedding and not a funeral service for this purpose. In other places of Scripture, we learn of the marriage at Cana and the preparation for the marriage supper of the Lamb. Marriage is a time of joy and happiness, and I believe that Jesus wants us to associate heaven with joy and happiness. The Christian life is to be filled with such joy.

> *"In Your presence is fullness of joy;*
> *at Your right hand are pleasures forevermore,"*
> *(Psalm 16: 11, NKJV).*

Sometimes, Christians give the impression that in order to make it to heaven a person has to surrender all her joys. Christianity is portrayed at times as a stern, stoic existence where laughter and joy are frowned upon. One brother in a church I visited for some time would start his greeting every Sabbath with the words, "Brethren, church is serious business!" We generally emphasize all the *don'ts* to our young people, thus giving the message that Jesus is a killjoy. The Christian lifestyle ought not to be presented as the destroyer of joy, but the guarantor of it.

We need to surrender only those transient destructive pleasures that rob us of our spiritual, moral and social development. It's no joy to be drowning in alcohol, shooting up drugs, racing police cars or creating mayhem on the streets after a Saturday night out. There are wholesome pleasures that build friendships, stimulate our higher powers and provide genuine relaxation with no hangovers.

The Ten Women Represent Christians

Please notice in the episode that all ten women were awaiting the coming of the bridegroom. In our context, therefore, we can safely say that they were all Christians. Furthermore, they all had lamps, and these were all lighted at the beginning. There was therefore no visible difference among the ten women. All were washed in the fountain, all were cleansed in the blood, all were awaiting the imminent arrival of their coming Lord.

This parable of the ten virgins, therefore, is not addressing the world at large, but the Christian church. We are not talking here about the un-churched, the openly disobedient, the villains or the rebels. This parable focuses upon the members of the family of God as they await the return of our Lord.

Are you waiting for your Bridegroom to come? Is the coming of Jesus the blessed hope of your heart? If it is, then you are represented here among the ten virgins. The number ten represents completeness, and thus these virgins can represent all Christians awaiting the second coming of Christ.

The Delay

Matthew 25:5 points out that the bridegroom was a long time in coming. It was the custom of the day for the waiting party to remain in readiness since the bridegroom may take some time to arrive. This delay could cause all sorts of difficulties. We have seen so much death, and sorrow, and sickness and pain. We have seen so much more injustice, inequalities, and oppression. Man's inhumanity to man continues to soar to new heights and befuddle our imaginations. Many Christians over the centuries have cried out in bitter agony, "O Lord Jesus, how long?"

This delay has also resulted in many who once walked with the Lord to begin to doubt and even scoff at the reality of the coming of Christ. Their walk with God moves down their scale of priorities and they begin to emphasize living only for the present world. I regard the delay as a test for the believer. It is the time when faith is tried. Living between the first and second advents of our Lord, between the already and the not yet, is a time of transition. Our faith is what bridges that gap between our entrance into the baptismal pool and our entrance into the banquet hall of the saved. It would be so easy to walk straight from one into the other. At the time of our conversion and baptism, we felt so close to the Lord. We wished then that we could have walked straight into the kingdom of glory where sin can no longer tempt us. But no! The Christian life is to be built and strengthened by faith for, *"without faith it is impossible to please Him,"* (Hebrews 11:6).

In the case of the ten women, the delay highlighted a major difference in their preparation for the arrival of the bridegroom. Five of them brought extra oil to keep their lamps alight, while the other five failed to make that preparation. The Bible thus describes the first group as wise and the second as foolish. You have got to keep your lamps bright and burning, no matter how long the wait. Irrespective of the difficulties that may assail you, of the challenges of your spiritual journey, you are to keep your lamps trimmed and burning. That's what we are to be doing here! We are all confronted in our spiritual walk with triumphs and tragedies, ups and downs, times of feasts and times of famine, but through it all, the Christian's imperative is ever to be looking *"for the Son of Man is coming in an hour you do not expect,"* (Matthew 24:44).

Keeping Faith Alive

The question, then, is how do we keep faith alive? How do we keep focused on the Lord's coming when the circumstances are foreboding; when the temptations are strong; when our lives are filled with problems that overwhelm and frustrate? How do we keep from throwing in the towel in our walk with God? What are we to do when trusting God does not seem to bring any immediate rewards?

The answer is found in *Galatians 5:22*. We are reminded there that faith is a fruit of the Spirit. Thus, in order for us to bear the fruit of faith, we must have the root of the Holy Spirit. Without the root, there will be no fruit. This is the key point of this parable. The wise virgins maintained their oil, symbolic of the Holy Spirit, through the delay. They had the extra oil that kept their faith alive and allowed them to be ready to enter into the marriage feast when the bridegroom finally arrived. The foolish women had no extra oil of the Spirit to keep their lamps trimmed and burning. Their oil went, and thus their faith, for *"If anyone does not have the Spirit of Christ, he is not His," (Romans 8:9)*.

Interestingly, however, there was no distinction between the wise and foolish virgins until the message came forth that the bridegroom was about to arrive. They all were dressed in white, they all had lamps and they all slumbered and slept. When the trumpet sounded, however, five were ready to go in while the other five came to recognize their lack. As a consequence, this latter group failed to make it into the marriage feast. While they maintained the outward show of preparedness (a lamp), they lacked the inner essential (oil).

These women had lamps without light; appearance without reality; form without function; vessels without value; symbols without significance. Sadly, no oil meant no entry to the banquet. I believe that this latter point is instructive for all Christians today. We may all be upholding the name of Christ. We may acknowledge His return at some point in the future, but if our faith is not kept alive through the presence of the Holy Spirit, we may be found wanting on that glorious day. We may also be guilty of maintaining the outward show of religiosity without the abiding presence of the Spirit of God. Despite the declaration that America is a Christian nation, we lament the rise in hate crimes, misogyny, mental and physical abuse, sexual immorality, and personal and corporate greed. As a country, we also have form without function, word without faith, ceremony without conviction, prayer without power, and church without Christ. The missing dimension is faith energized by the Holy Spirit of God.

We should pause to take stock of our spiritual condition so that we might determine whether all is well. The question *Why are you here?* must be seriously reflected upon and satisfactorily answered on an ongoing basis to avoid any self-delusion. It is so easy to march to the drums of our ideology, our politics, our religion, or our gang. We may even be holding full-time clergy positions as ministers, directors and presidents, and yet have no spiritual oil burning within. I see people caught up in the religio-political dynamics of their denomination. They have mastered the keys for surviving and thriving in that milieu. They may gain earthly plaudits and scale denominational heights, but while there is nothing wrong with earthly accolades, if they come at the price of a place in God's eternal kingdom, then the cost is too great.

> "For what profit is it to a man if he gains the whole world, and loses his own soul?" (Matthew 16:26).

The Work of the Holy Spirit

We hear little about the work of the Holy Spirit in the life of a Christian, but the Holy Spirit is the Person of the Godhead that enables us today to live the life of Christ. It is the Spirit within that enables us to keep going when we feel like giving up. It is the Spirit within that enables us to turn the other cheek, to be at peace in the midst of the storm, to engage in totally selfless acts of mercy and love, to find spiritual enrichment in church and in the company of fellow believers. When the Holy Spirit is not valued or appreciated, there is spiritual drought, darkness, declension and death. The Scriptures are replete with counsel encouraging us to be filled with the Spirit of God.

Let the Spirit fill your life — Ephesians 5: 18

Receive the Holy Spirit — John 20:22

*People who don't have the Spirit of Christ
in them don't belong to Him
— Romans 8:9*

Follow the Spirit — Galatians 5: 25

*Your body is a temple where the Holy Spirit dwells
— 1 Corinthians 6: 19*

The good news is that the presence and power of the Holy Spirit is available to every believer. Like Christ, at our baptism we are endowed with the gift of the Spirit. However, the Spirit cannot coexist with premeditated sin in the life. The more we surrender our lives to the will of Christ, the closer we come to partaking of His divine nature, and the more His Spirit is able to reign within us.

Some Christians teach that the evidence of the Spirit in a life is the ability to speak in tongues. Such a conclusion is drawn because of a misunderstanding between a gift and a fruit. The Bible teaches that the ability to speak in tongues is a gift of the spirit. A gift is freely given and is selective–some receive it and others don't. There is nothing punitive or sinful about not receiving a gift. Indeed, the Bible points out that various gifts are distributed by the Holy Spirit. These include speaking in tongues, healing, administration, evangelism, pastoring, teaching, and so forth. *Ephesians 4: 11* reminds us that these are all given to build up the body of Christ. On the other hand, *Galatians 5: 22* tells us that *"the fruit of the Spirit is love, joy, peace, long-suffering, gentleness, goodness, faith, meekness, temperance."*

Every Christian who has the *root* of the Spirit in his/her life will demonstrate the *fruit* of the Spirit as listed above. If you have the root, you will bear the fruit. When the Spirit is in control of your life, you will see the fruit of love, gentleness, faith, peace, long-suffering and temperance. Do not look to those who rise up in an emotional frenzy, sputter mixtures of incoherent syllables and echo almost deafening words of so-called praise to God as the ones who have the Holy Spirit. Look rather to their dealings with their loved ones, their neighbors, and their daily walk with God in the marketplace of life. These provide the bona fide evidence of His presence in the life. The prayer of such persons is that of the hymn-writer: "O *let me walk with thee my God, as Enoch walked in days of old,"* ("Walking with God.")

The Spirit as Companion

What does the Spirit do in our lives? How does He contribute to keeping faith alive? He fulfills several functions. First, He serves as our constant Companion. *Matthew 28:20* is fulfilled with the outpouring of the Holy Spirit in the life of the believer. *"I will be with you always."*

We have the assurance, as children of God, that we are never left alone to face the vicissitudes of life. Our God has promised to be with us through the Holy Spirit.

"I may walk through valleys as dark as death, but I won't be afraid. You are with me, and your shepherd's rod makes me feel safe," (Psalm 23:4).

Through the prophet Isaiah, the Lord comforts us:

"Don't be afraid. I am with you. Don't tremble with fear. I am your God," (Isaiah 41:10).

The Spirit as Guide and Counselor

Secondly, the Spirit serves as our Guide and Counselor. He guides us into all truth. He convicts us of sin, righteousness and of the judgment to come. The Lord, speaking through the psalmist David, states that *"I will point out the road that you should follow. I will be your teacher and watch over you," (Psalm 32:8).*

The Spirit as Comforter

Thirdly, the Holy Spirit serves as our Comforter. When days are dark and dreary; when loneliness and depression fill the life; when all seems lost and gone; the Spirit is there to comfort and cheer us. We all go through our Mini-Gethsemanes, but it is so comforting at those times to have the inner voice of the

Holy Spirit strengthening us, allowing us to make it through another day.

The Spirit as Enabler

Fourthly, the Spirit serves as our Enabler. He empowers us both to live daily for Christ and to testify to His name. Through His enabling power we are able to manifest the fruit of the Spirit in our lives, making us nice to be near. Our lives are filled with love, joy, peace and goodness because of the work of the Holy Spirit.

The Spirit Gives Power to Witness

Finally, we are told: *"But the Holy Spirit will come upon you and give you power. Then you will tell everyone about me," (Acts 1:8).*

The Spirit gives us power to witness boldly for the name of Christ. I grew up a naturally shy and reserved person, yet I have seen how God has used me to speak to large audiences and glorify His name. That has only been possible because of the empowering work of His Holy Spirit. There is a holy boldness that comes to the Christian when s/he seeks to uplift Christ. *Are you led by His Holy Spirit?*

The parable of the ten virgins concludes with five wise and prepared women on the inside and five unprepared women on the outside shouting at a locked door to let them in. What a sad scene! We are then admonished to be watchful since we do not know the hour of our Lord's appearing. The issue is not merely the destination, but the journey. If we make it to our heavenly destination, it will be because we have maintained our faith in Jesus through the ministry of His Holy Spirit on our life's journey. We are to be prepared now so that we will be ready then.

Of course, the journey has joys all its own. Even without a heaven to gain at the end of the road, it still makes sense to walk the Christian's pathway. It's still the best way to live in the here and now. Love is always to be preferred to indifference or hate; peace is always to be preferred to war; faith to fear. Then, marvelous grace, we have heaven on top of all that! My only cry now has to be, Lord, fill me with your Holy Spirit! That's my prayer while I'm here on this earth.

CHAPTER FIFTEEN

TROUBLE WON'T LAST

One of the most difficult assignments I have had in my ministerial career thus far has been to officiate at the funeral service of a dear friend, colleague and former ministerial intern. John was snuffed out in the prime of his career, leaving a young wife and a teenaged son. He was in the Lord's work and a long, bright future seemed ahead. But it was not to be! What do you say on such occasions?

At the service, we sang hymns of thanksgiving and praise. I preached a sermon of comfort and hope. "How are you coping?" I inquired of his wife.

Ann's response was so reassuring. "I am coping by the grace of God!"

Over the years, I have kept in touch with Ann and her son Heylon and it's always such a joy to see how they have maintained their calm, yet resolute trust in God. I conducted Heylon's wedding, saw the birth and growth of his lovely children, and saw Ann retire from a long career in nursing. I see in that family the words of the hymn-writer, "*Be not dismayed, whate'er betide God will take care of you,"* ("Be Not Dismayed Whate'er Betide.")

What enables us to sing in the face of trouble? What allows a bereaved wife to avoid descending into abject bewilderment at a future without a husband, but instead say, "I am coping by the grace of God"? What keeps us from stabbing our fingers at the face of God, at the hurt and pain, the crying injustices and abuses that we encounter personally or professionally? What allows us to solemnly consent to serve Him whatever the consequences? What enables the Christian to sing with conviction and peaceful assurance in the face of death?

I believe that *John 14: 1-3* provides some answers. Jesus begins His discourse with this declarative assurance: *"Don't be worried! Have faith in God and have faith in me."*

This suggests that it is possible for the Christian to worry. We are not exempt from the troubles that afflict all humanity, but we are counseled not to worry about them. *Job 14: 1-2* says: *"Life is short and sorrowful for every living soul. We are flowers that fade and shadows that vanish."*

In *John 16:33* we are told: *"While you are in the world, you will have to suffer. But cheer up! I have defeated the world."*

Jesus Himself said in *Matthew 6:34: "Don't worry about tomorrow. It will take care of itself. You have enough to worry about today."*

We are all students in life's university of trouble, and at times we are severely tested there. I am so comforted by the encouraging words of our Lord, *"Don't be worried! Have faith in God and have faith in me."* There may be trouble all around you, but it does not have to depress and frustrate you. While it may get at you, it does not have to get to you. Jesus' declaration assures us not to be troubled by trouble, no matter what the nature of that trouble.

When Jesus uttered these words to His disciples, they had just heard that Peter would deny Jesus, Judas would betray Him, and that Jesus was going to be put to death. Yet, in the midst of all their confusion and grief, Jesus says to them, *"Don't be worried!"* Jesus was not talking here about weeping for, in our humanity, tears do flow and indeed, should when the pain of the effects of sin is seen. Even our Lord wept at the passing of His beloved friend, Lazarus. Weeping is wholesome and therapeutic — we should never bottle up our tears. While the tears flow, however, the heart remains firm, trusting and assured in a God who is in absolute control. The heart here refers to the mind, the seat of reason and decision-making. It's a rational, intellectual choice that one makes not to be troubled by trouble.

The application of this counsel is best demonstrated in the experience of Job in the Old Testament. In swift succession, Job got reports of the destruction of his land and livestock, the death of his children and the doubts of his own wife as to the goodness of God. He struggled to deal with all the calamities, as the world seemed to be closing in on him. Yet, in the midst of these traumatic times, he summoned that spiritual energy and faith to proclaim in *Job 19:25, 26*: *"I know that my Protector lives, and at the end he will stand on this earth. My flesh may be destroyed, yet from this body I will see God."*

Beyond the hurt feelings and grieved emotions, there is in the child *of* God a conviction that affirms that the Lord God Omnipotent reigns and He does all things well. We may not understand all now, but we still stand under His will, since we believe that God is good to us all the time.

"The Lord gives perfect peace to those whose faith is firm. So always trust the Lord because he is forever our mighty rock," (Isaiah 26:3-4).

This trust in God is a bulwark that keeps the child of God despite the pain and tears. What we are talking about here is the essence of the Christian's faith. This belief lies at the foundation of the Christian's walk with God for, without faith, no one can please Him *(Hebrews 11:6)*. This faith enables me to trust my life to the control of the Spirit of God. This brings a peace, an equanimity of spirit, a calm assurance, a blessed trust that whatever transpires, it is well. Thus, your heart remains at rest even as you are in the midst of your personal storms.

> "You give peace of mind to all who love your Law. Nothing can make them fall," (Psalm 119:165).

> *Peace, perfect peace While in this world of sin*
> *The blood of Jesus whispers peace within*
> ("Peace, Perfect Peace, in This Dark World of Sin?").

It is a joyous experience for the person whose life is in Christ. When you accept Him as your Savior, even though you continue to walk in time, you are really living in eternity. The future rushes into our present and superimposes itself upon our natural human responses.

In *verses 2-3 of John 14,* Jesus gave us an incontrovertible reason why we should not be troubled by trouble here on earth. The reality is that it won't last. He promises to return and take us to homes in glory where sin does not abound, where affliction shall not rise a second time, and where none shall say, "I am sick." *"I am going there to prepare a place for each of you. After I* have done this, I will come back and take you with me. Then we will be together." In Revelation 21, John saw the glorious vision of a new heaven and a new earth, for the first earth had disappeared. In that land, John says, there will be no more sorrow, no crying or pain, for these things of the past are gone forever.

Let us therefore lift up the trumpets and sing joyfully for He is coming once again to set His people free. We see so much pain and misery around us. Our loved ones are ravaged by cancer, AIDS, heart problems and other maladies of the human experience. We see so much instability in our political and economic arenas, we see so much suffering brought on by man-made and natural disasters but thank God we can sing and shout that trouble won't last.

David Wilson was a friend and a minister that I admired. He ran six miles every morning, lived a health-conscious life and generally lived to the glory of God. He would chide me at times for my failure to pursue a more consistent exercise regime and, admitting my guilt, I often promised him to do better. David and his wife Gurley were close friends of ours, and our families exchanged visits on a regular basis. I particularly loved to visit their home, since Gurley made a roti and curry that was absolutely mouth-watering.

David started feeling ill and made several trips to various doctors and the hospital. After months of testing, the diagnosis was finally made. David had stage 4 prostate cancer, and he was expected to die within a few months. The news devastated us. I visited David at the hospital and saw him wasting away as the cancer devoured his body, but I thank God for his last words to me. He said, "Clinton, we as ministers talk faith and preach faith, but it is only when you reach my condition that you know what faith in God really is!" I believe that he died in Christ, looking by faith to a better tomorrow with Christ when He comes.

There is coming a time when there will be no need for doctors, hospitals or funeral parlors. There will be no need for the police, the prisons or the political system. There will be no hatred, crime or violence. Thank God, there will be no racism, oppression or injustice. Our loving Lord gives us faith to bear our ills now and the faith to hold on until that glorious, brighter day.

> *"What God has planned for people who love him
> is more than eyes have seen or ears have heard.
> It has never even entered our minds!"*
> *(1 Corinthians 2:9).*

Therefore, let us all look forward to that amazing day when all God's people will forever be with their Lord. I'm here patiently living, loving, learning, and looking forward to the joyous and eternal good times that are ahead. I want to spend eternity with my Jesus, don't you?

CHAPTER SIXTEEN

FROM VISION TO VICTORY

From Vision to Victory was the theme chosen for a camp meeting of the South Atlantic Conference where I served as a pastor. Many speakers, including myself, explored the challenges facing the church as we live in these end-times of earth's history. The final scenes of earth's drama are fast changing, mind boggling and stupendous in their significance. How are we, as Christians and as a Christian community, to respond to all the myriad of life-changing events that confront us on a daily basis?

Our challenge is to retain our vision of our life's purpose. In the midst of changing traditional values and norms regarding gender, sexuality, alternative lifestyles, and other social issues, how can the Christian and the Christian church preserve biblical truth and maintain a hopeful and expectant focus as we await the glorious victorious return of Christ? This is a major challenge facing the Christian community today, and I must confess the overall signs are not hopeful. Matthew predicts that in the last days, *"false messiahs and false prophets will come and work great miracles and signs. They will even try to fool God's chosen one,"* (Matthew 24:24). We are confronted with so many new realities in our political, economic and social arenas that we are challenged to assess the incoming against our traditional views and our biblical understandings. Many well-meaning Christians and Christian communities listen to and support such progressive thinking and realities and are advocating a different course for our world. It is critical for sincere Christians today to recognize the realities of our changing world, but to remain rooted on the foundation pillars of the Christian faith and our enduring mission to proclaim the everlasting gospel of our Lord. I want to elaborate on these two points and then conclude with the joyous results effective, transformative ministry will produce in the closing days of earth's history and the ultimate drama of the ages — the return of Christ.

THE REALITIES OF A CHANGING WORLD

Charles Dickens, the famous English author, described the context of a particular historic period in English-French relations with these words: "It was the best of times; it was the worst of times," (*A Quote from A Tale of Two Cities*.). This may well be an apt description of our times, for our society today is exposed to many comforts but these are accompanied by so many curses.

Even a blind man in dark sunglasses on a dark night, looking for a lost coin which he never had, could see that our world is changing rapidly, radically and fundamentally. Our traditional values, morals, ways of thinking and doing, are all coming into headlong collision with the new world order. As Alvin Toffler predicted many years ago in *Future Shock,* the only constant phenomenon is change.

Highlights of Major Changes
Common currency
There are several major changes taking place that will have a serious impact on the way we live. The countries of Western Europe have banded themselves together into a monetary union and the euro is now their common unit of currency. Discussions are taking place in the Unites States as to whether one world currency is a feasible option. The advent of digital currency makes such a possibility that much easier to imagine and realize.

Cashless Society
There is also the consideration of moving to a cashless society where a microchip containing your relevant details is implanted under your skin. You will then only have to swipe your hand at checkout points and all your account information would be maintained on a central server. Is this what John spoke about in *Revelation 13: 1?* He refers to that beast power that forced everyone to receive a mark in his hand or in his forehead and that no one could buy or sell except those that had the mark. I have no conclusive evidence as to what would constitute the mark of the beast, but these trends are worthy of note.

AI and Other Technology Innovations
Another major feature of our changing society is the reality associated with AI technology. While this advanced technology has tremendous power for good, its potential for misinformation and disinformation is quite a disturbing reality. Joy Reid, an MSNBC anchor, was reported to have been interviewed by CNN anchor Anderson Cooper, where she was promoting a product to enhance fitness. The video images and the audio were of these two television personalities, but the reality was

that these two had never met and never had such an interview. It was all the product of AI technology, used to promote disinformation. In another case, an Ohio mother heard her daughter's voice on the phone telling her that she had been kidnapped and her captors were demanding a ransom from her parents. The truth was that the daughter was not captured but was safe and sound at a friend's house, totally unaware of the phone call to her mother!

Recent research has documented that there is less communication in homes now since more time is spent in front of technology devices. As the use of the internet for business expands, this trend is bound to increase. You no longer share a light moment with your office colleague at the water fountain, but rather you chat online. It's not unusual for family members to communicate with one another online even when they are in the same room!

Recognizing the deep relational needs of the human spirit — the need to love and be loved, to communicate verbally and non-verbally, and to express warmth and closeness — the current technological shifts in communication bring both a challenge and an opportunity for a warm, caring Christian community. We need to be intentional in ensuring that the need for human interactions that are warm, engaging, and emotionally satisfying are not lost. High touch must accompany our modern high skill technological advancements if we are to continue to demonstrate the fruits of the Spirit shared by the apostle Paul in Galatians 5.

Valueless Society

A fourth feature I wish to highlight is our steady descent into what I regard as a valueless society. Propelled by our current political and social climate, Hollywood, the print and television media, our society is now pushing back the frontiers of truth, decency and moral acceptability before our very eyes. Societal views on drug abuse, the use of guns, and honesty and integrity in politics, business and our personal lives have all become more relaxed and liberal. You may now do whatever you wish in your personal life, and it is to be accepted by others, for you are now the sole judge on behavioral practices.

As I write, the former President of the United States, Donald Trump, has been indicted in four different jurisdictions, and faces other lawsuits. Nevertheless, his popularity ratings continue to climb, especially among evangelical Christians. Meanwhile, he professes his innocence on all counts. The final judgment on his cases is left to the judicial system, but it's new territory for our country and our world when a former president is alleged to have committed so many abuses of power and privilege. Of course, many remain stoutly in his defense. Accusations of fraud, the stealing of elections, extremist ideologies, and conspiracy theories abound. Only time will tell how this saga in American life ends, but the impact on traditional Christian morals and values is incalculable.

REQUIREMENTS FROM A CHANGING WORLD

As a Christian community, what should we do, given the realities of our changing world? How can the Christian church remain relevant, contextual, and yet biblically consistent in our changing society so that it may remain a beacon of hope amidst the shoals of truth deficits and moral degradation? Permit me to share what I regard as three prime requirements that our society demands from the church.

Maintain Biblical Standards

Irrespective of the moral and spiritual slide, the Christian community is still expected to promote and maintain clear, uncompromising biblical standards. If the church is to continue to be recognized and valued as a worthwhile institution in society, then it must remain true and consistent to its biblical mandate. When society says everybody is breaking the rules, the church ought to be still saying nobody ought to break the rules. When society winks at actions borne out of expediency and malfeasance, the church must be ever unequivocal in challenging us to act from fixed principles. The church must retain its moral fiber, its authority to declare the truth of God and to call men and women to order their lives in harmony with that truth.

Despite the moral decadence in our society, the Christian church must still proclaim that it is good to love God, to honor parents, and to avoid actions that benumb our senses, belittle others, or besmirch reputations. No matter how much the world changes, these bedrock principles and values must remain, and the Christian church is the one institution in society that is charged with the responsibility of preserving the true north of our moral and spiritual compass.

Practice What You Preach

Secondly, our society expects that Christian standards must come alive in real people. We *must* live what we preach, possess what we profess, and *walk* what we talk. In a world filled with double dealing, backstabbing, ruthless conniving and abject greed, church members and leaders must be viewed as honest, open, transparent, caring and truthful. The Christian community is sadly discredited when our leaders are found guilty of major crimes such as embezzlement, fraud and scandalous moral indiscretions. On the other hand, it is such a joy to find Christians who are daily walking with their Lord and living Christian values. What a joy it is to find Christians who can pray for us and with us as spontaneously as they can breathe, and who can offer spiritual support to those who are experiencing difficulties in their lives. We need Christians who can act as a saving moral influence in our society.

"Make your light shine, so others will see the good you do and will praise your Father in heaven," (Matthew 5:16).

Maintain Mission-Driven Church Congregations

Thirdly, our society requires Christ-centered, mission-driven, user-friendly church congregations. A Christian church must make a difference in its community. It was especially noticeable to me during my 13 years of ministry in Europe how many churches had closed and been converted into factories and warehouses. While church attendance is still popular in the United States, although less so after the COVID pandemic, the level of attendance has not always been accompanied by a corresponding level of godly living and sharing of the faith. For many, the spiritual dimension has been obliterated from their church attendance and going to church has become little more than a meaningless religious duty or routine.

In *1 Chronicles 12*, we read of men from various tribes who came to join David's army at Ziklag. There were sons of Kish — mighty men who could hurl stones equally well with either their left or right hands. There were the Gadites–men whose faces were like the faces of lions and who were as swift as deer upon the mountains. It was indeed a mighty army filled with men of might and valor. Among the company of soldiers, we read in *verse 32* that there were the children of Issachar. These were leaders who knew the right time to do what needed to be done. They were planners, strategists, and change agents who moved as a united force. The church today needs valiant and committed foot soldiers, but the demands of our changing world also require the church to have strategic and visionary leaders and members who understand the times in which we live and can pilot the church through these challenging times.

The ministry of the Christian church must be to all people, for our God is an all-inclusive God. We are to minister to the youth and the aged, the singles and the marrieds, the widowed and the divorced, the accomplished Ph.Ds., and the aspiring GEDs. The church is to reach out beyond its normal comfort zone to touch the lives of the LGBTQIA+ community as well as drug addicts, prostitutes and prisoners. Its message is to reach out to people of all nationalities and socio-economic standings. Brown or yellow, black or white — all are precious in His sight. The methods of ministry would be dictated by the target group being addressed, for there can be no one-size-fits-all approach to reaching others. Methods need to be relevant to the specific audience and must change with time. Please note that I am talking about methods, not the message. The Christian message is clear and unchanging, but methods need to be contextual. The methods must change; the message cannot. Structures must change to suit the milieu; standards cannot. Policies and practices must change for continuing relevance; bedrock principles cannot.

One of the major criticisms of the traditional, conservative Christian church has been its unresponsiveness to change. While we dare not throw away the foundations of our assurance and hope, or our distinctive fundamentals that have kept and guided us over the centuries, yet the church must be responsive to changes in methodology. If the church is to remain viable and relevant in the 21st century, changes must take place. Yesterday's ways, yesterday's methods, and yesterday's thinking will not be effective in meeting the needs of the current and future generations. We cannot continue the way we always did and expect success. Our technology, our *modus operandi*, must change with time.

FROM VISION TO VICTORY

The Christian church is destined to triumph. How do I know? Well, I have read the end of the book. Students of Bible prophecies support the fact that the coming of Jesus cannot be too far away. The sins of the times are nothing, but signs of the times and they indicate in no uncertain terms the footsteps of an approaching God. Soon, the last sermon will have been preached; soon, the last religious meeting will have been conducted; soon, the last food basket will have been distributed; the last tract given away; the last church elections held; for He that shall come will come and will not tarry. Then, the divine edict of *Revelation 22: 11* will be uttered as humanity is sealed for eternal happiness or ultimate destruction: *"He who is unjust, let him be unjust still; he who is filthy let him be filthy still; he who is righteous, let him be righteous still; he who is holy, let him be holy still," (NKJV)*.

The final movements of this earth's history are going to be rapid ones. Soon, the trumpets shall sound and the dead in Christ shall be raised. At the same moment, the living righteous will be translated to meet their Lord in the air. What a glorious day that will be when the saints of all ages and from all ages are finally united with their Lord. John's description in *Revelation 19: 1-6* fills me with unspeakable joy. The saints of God with one voice will shout and sing, "Hallelujah." They praise God, for the Lord Omnipotent reigns.

In the midst of such glorious global realities so soon to be fulfilled, the question is therefore pertinent: *Why are you here?* The victory of the people of God is assured, for the Bible is clear on this matter. The real issue is whether we, as individuals, will be part of that victorious throng.

In this book, I have endeavored to point out that by adequately responding to the important philosophical question, *why are you here?* in terms of our living, loving, learning and looking, we will be able to chart a victorious course through this life and ultimately be with our Lord when He comes. Therefore, the call today is to surrender our lives to the will of God, to live as His Word prescribes, to love as He loves, to learn more about Him and His lofty aspirations for us and to look forward to His return in glory.

When we become responsive to His bidding, as found in His Word, ours will be the joy of being part of the church militant that triumphs at the coming of Jesus. A mansion in glory and permanent citizenship in the eternal home of the saved will be our destiny. *Why are you here,* you ask? Well, I am here to daily live, love, learn and look as a Christian should, glorifying my God, benefiting my society and getting ready to be a part of His eternal family. *That's a glorious life purpose, isn't it?*

Epilogue

Putting it all together!

Why are you here? is a probing devotional, inviting you to re-think your life's purpose from a biblical, Judeo-Christian perspective. It challenges the reader to look at life through the lens of a four-part life symphony: to live, to learn, to love, and to look. Above all, it advocates for living a life driven by purpose – a purpose arising from one's relationship with God.

I have taught my doctoral students at the University of the Virgin Islands that life is a business. I am the CEO of Me, Inc. My life is my business, and as with any business, it ought to be growing, driven by vision, mission, and values. All life's decisions are to be made in the context of furthering my life's purpose under God. As a responsible adult, as with any other business, I may receive advice, guidance, and support from other sources, but ultimately, my life's decisions are to be made based on my convictions and my sense of God's will for me.

As a leadership educator, I looked to the discipline for a theoretical framework for this perspective. I found support in the theory of integrative leadership. Integrative leadership is a holistic approach to leading yourself and others in a reflective, conscious, and responsive way according to your vision, mission and values. Often described as holistic leadership, it speaks to the development of a leader in all dimensions: physical, psychological, emotional, intellectual, and spiritual. It is a moral and spiritual journey whose guiding compass is found within a leader's soul (Dhiman, S. 2018).

The literature on integrative leadership provides a helpful framework to connect the themes of my life as a business, of making choices based on my life's purpose and values, and of operating from a moral and spiritual compass. That's essentially what this book is about. The sound principles of self-motivation, creativity and innovation, emotional intelligence, spiritual intelligence, optimal performance, and fulfillment are all present in this holistic understanding of integrative leadership.

Integrative leadership encourages us to expect the best of ourselves and from ourselves so that we could become all that we can be. Blaming others for how our life is going is not helpful, for we are responsible for the choices we make and the consequences that result. Integrative leadership speaks to our responsibility and our accountability for our decisions and actions.

Integrative leaders live lives of purpose, meaning and connection; make positive contributions to the people, teams, organizations and communities they serve; and experience a joy in the journey of life. There will be obstacles, frustrations, and myriad challenges along the way, but as Chief Executive of Me, Inc., with God as your Guide, yours is the privilege of surmounting these negatives and leading your life with joy, meaning, and purpose. That's why you are here!

References

"All to Jesus I Surrender," n.d. https://www.hymnal.net/en/hymn/h/441.

"A Quote by Walter D. Wintle," n.d. https://www.goodreads.com/quotes/1033193-if-you-think-you-are-beaten-you-are-if-you.

"A Quote from A Tale of Two Cities," n.d. https://www.goodreads.com/quotes/341391-it-was-the-best-of-times-it-was-the-worst.

"Andraé Crouch–Take Me Back Lyrics | Lyrics. Com," n.d. https://www.lyrics.com/lyric/29033/Andra%C3%A9+Crouch/Take+Me+Back.

"Be Not Dismayed Whate'er Betide," n.d. https://www.hymnal.net/en/hymn/h/694.

Chemers, M. 1997. *An Integrative Theory of Leadership.* Routledge.

"Christ's Object Lessons," n.d. https://m.egwwritings.org/en/book/15.221.

"Counsels on Stewardship," n.d. https://m.egwwritings.org/en/book/22.98.

Dhiman, S. 2018. *Holistic Leadership: A New Paradigm for Fulfilled Leaders.* Palgrave Macmillan. Dhiman, S. (eds). 2018. *Engaged Leadership. Management for Professionals.* Springer.

"E.G. White, 'Testimonies for the Church Volume Three,'" n.d. https://www.gilead.net/egw/books/testimonies/Testimonies_for_the_Church_Volume_Three/index.htm.

"Ellen G. White Estate: Daily Devotional–With God at Dawn," n.d., https://whiteestate.org/devotional/wgd/09_17/#:~:text=%E2% 80%94Patriarchs%20and%20Prophets%2C%20290.,as%20co%2Dworkers%20with%20Him.

Fisher, J. 2016. *A Thoughtful Leader: A Model of Integrative Leadership.* Rotman-UTP Publishing.

Gaither, Bill, "It Is No Secret–Bill Gaither," SongLyrics.com, n.d., https://www.songlyrics.com/bill-gaither/it-is-no-secret-lyrics/.

Hatala, J. and Hatala, L. 2005. *Integrative Leadership.* Integrative Leadership Institute.

"Hope for Dying Marriages," n.d. https://dobsonlibrary.com/resource/article/047d6944-3aa6-4719-9091-49c7a91744ad.

Hymnary.org. "Anywhere with Jesus," n.d. https://hymnary.org/text/anywhere_with_jesus_i_can_safely_go.

Hymnary.org. "I Gave My Life for Thee," n.d. https://hymnary.org/text/i_gave_my_life_for_thee.

Hymnary.org. "Peace, Perfect Peace, in This Dark World of Sin?," n.d. https://hymnary.org/text/peace_perfect_peace_in_this_dark_world_o.

Hymnary.org. "Walking with God," n.d. https://hymnary.org/text/o_let_me_walk_with_thee_my_God.

I Know the Lord Will Make a Way for Me Chords–Twila Paris. "I Know The Lord Will Make A Way For Me Chords–Twila Paris," July 14, 2022. https://www.psalmnote.com/song/i-know-the-lord-will-make-a-way-for-me-chords-twila-paris.

Keller, Werner. 1983. *The Bible as History*. Bantam.

Naisbitt, John. Megatrends. Warner Books, 1984, p. 36.

Poetry Foundation. "Sonnet 116: Let Me Not to the Marriage of True… | Poetry Foundation," n.d. https://www.poetryfoundation.org/poems/45106/sonnet-116-let-me-not-to-the-marriage-of-true-minds.

Printed in the USA
CPSIA information can be obtained
at www.ICGtesting.com
CBHW040749201223
2790CB00007B/146